Funded

The Entrepreneur's Guide to Raising Your First Round

Katherine Hague

Beijing · Boston · Farnham · Sebastopol · Tokyo

Funded

by Katherine Hague

Copyright © 2017 Katherine Hague. All rights reserved.

Printed in the United States of America.

Published by O'Reilly Media, Inc., 1005 Gravenstein Highway North, Sebastopol, CA 95472.

O'Reilly books may be purchased for educational, business, or sales promotional use. Online editions are also available for most titles (*http://safaribooksonline.com*). For more information, contact our corporate/institutional sales department: 800-998-9938 or *corporate@oreilly.com*.

Editors: Susan Conant and Jeff Bleiel
Production Editor: Kristen Brown
Copyeditor: Rachel Monaghan
Proofreader: Rachel Head

Indexer: Angela Howard
Interior Designer: David Futato
Cover Designer: Edie Freedman
Illustrator: Rebecca Demarest

October 2016:   First Edition

Revision History for the First Edition

2016-09-19:   First Release

See *http://oreilly.com/catalog/errata.csp?isbn=9781491940266* for release details.

978-1-491-94026-6

[LSI]

Table of Contents

Part III. Executing Your Fundraise

9. The Investor Pipeline. 97

Preface

Why Funded?

In this book, you'll learn what it takes to successfully raise a round of funding for your company.

The venture capital (VC) world is often intimidating and can be hard to navigate, even for the most seasoned entrepreneurs. The good news is that it doesn't have to be. Entrepreneurs who run a successful fundraising process don't do it by accident. This book will prepare you to fundraise like the best. It will help you build a foundational knowledge of how the venture capital industry works, and walk you through each step of planning, executing, and optimizing a fundraise of your own. *Funded* is packed full of exercises, checklists, and templates that will guide you through the fundraising process, start to finish.

Reading this book before you step out onto the fundraising trail will save you time and prepare you to fundraise with confidence. The purpose of this book is to enhance your prospects for achieving and exceeding your fundraising goals.

Is This Book for You?

Funded acts as a road map for all entrepreneurs in their quest to secure seed capital. This book is meant to be a handbook for the road warriors—the founders who will be knocking on doors to raise capital to grow their businesses.

Funded has lessons for entrepreneurs of all levels of experience. Veteran entrepreneurs will refresh their knowledge while honing their fundraising strategies. Entrepreneurs inexperienced in fundraising will learn what it takes to raise a round of capital from the ground up.

While *Funded* is written first and foremost for entrepreneurs raising their first round of capital, many of its lessons are timeless startup principles. Entrepreneurs raising later rounds of capital, entrepreneurs who aren't sure how to finance their businesses, early-stage employees, and investors will all benefit from the information provided in this book.

You're in the right place if you are:

- A startup founder
- A small business owner considering equity financing
- A C-level employee at an early-stage company
- An aspiring entrepreneur
- An early-stage investor
- Anyone else who wants an authoritative overview of the startup fundraising process

By reading this book you'll:

- Gain an understanding of core venture capital concepts and standards
- Learn to develop and hone an investor pitch
- Come away with a plan to hit the fundraising trail for your company
- Develop the confidence to negotiate key terms in a funding deal
- Understand best practices in fundraising today

What You'll Find Inside

Funded has been divided into four sections, covering everything you need to know as you set out to raise your first round:

Part I

The first section builds a foundational knowledge of core topics relating to venture capital. It will help you understand when and why to raise money from investors, discuss the alternatives to venture capital, and introduce you to the core principles of ownership and valuation.

Part II

The second section will prepare you for the fundraising trail. We'll discuss what investors will be looking for from your company and what you'll need to develop before you make your first pitch. From pitch decks to financial projections and what to expect during the due diligence process, we cover it all here.

Part III

The third section is all about execution. We'll go through each step of the fundraising process, from structuring your fundraising to finding investors to getting money in the bank. When to raise capital, how much to raise, how to structure your deal, and what it takes to close the deal: we go through it all here.

Part IV

The fourth and final section of *Funded* is our Top Tens. Here we go through the top 10 mistakes founders make when raising their first round and dive into equity crowdfunding strategies and fundraising hacks.

TheEntrepreneursGuide.com

In addition to the interactive exercises and checklists included throughout the book, we've developed a companion website packed with more resources to help you succeed. Visit *TheEntrepreneursGuide.com* to download templates, check out additional content, and access support from the *Funded* community.

Safari® Books Online

Safari Books Online is an on-demand digital library that delivers expert content in both book and video form from the world's leading authors in technology and business.

Technology professionals, software developers, web designers, and business and creative professionals use Safari Books Online as their primary resource for research, problem solving, learning, and certification training.

Safari Books Online offers a range of plans and pricing for enterprise, government, education, and individuals.

Members have access to thousands of books, training videos, and prepublication manuscripts in one fully searchable database from publishers like O'Reilly Media, Prentice Hall Professional, Addison-Wesley Professional, Microsoft Press, Sams, Que, Peachpit Press, Focal Press, Cisco Press, John Wiley & Sons, Syngress, Morgan Kaufmann, IBM Redbooks, Packt, Adobe Press, FT Press, Apress, Manning, New Riders,

McGraw-Hill, Jones & Bartlett, Course Technology, and hundreds more. For more information about Safari Books Online, please visit us online.

How to Contact Us

Please address comments and questions concerning this book to the publisher:

O'Reilly Media, Inc.
1005 Gravenstein Highway North
Sebastopol, CA 95472
800-998-9938 (in the United States or Canada)
707-829-0515 (international or local)
707-829-0104 (fax)

We have a web page for this book, where we list errata, examples, and any additional information. You can access this page at *http://bit.ly/ funded_1e*.

To comment or ask technical questions about this book, send email to *bookquestions@oreilly.com*.

For more information about our books, courses, conferences, and news, see our website at *http://www.oreilly.com*.

Find us on Facebook: *http://facebook.com/oreilly*
Follow us on Twitter: *http://twitter.com/oreillymedia*
Watch us on YouTube: *http://www.youtube.com/oreillymedia*

Acknowledgments

A special thank you goes out to Roger Chabra of Rho Canada Ventures and David Crow for their guidance and support in reviewing early drafts of *Funded*.

PART I

Building a Foundational Knowledge

CHAPTER 1

What Makes a Startup Fundable?

So you want to raise money for your startup?

Before you decide if you should raise money, it is important to understand that not every company is fundable.

Fundable, for our purposes, means that your company is attractive to investors that provide growth capital to high-risk, high-growth-potential, early-stage ventures. This type of capital is generally referred to as *venture capital*, and can be provided by both professional investors (venture capitalists) and private individuals (angel investors).

Venture capital can be provided in exchange for equity (an ownership share in the company) or in exchange for debt. Not every company is attractive as a venture capital investment. Less than 25% of all startup funding is done through venture capital, either in the form of friends and family funding (24%) or through professional venture capital firms (1%) (*http://on.mktw.net/2cCmiWM*). Companies that don't raise capital self-fund, or use alternate forms of capital covered in the next chapter.

How Investors Make Money

Your investors, and you, will make money when your company reaches a successful liquidity event. A liquidity event is something that converts an investor's equity in your company into cash. The most common liquidity event is an acquisition, where a company is acquired by another company or private equity firm. Investors can also see liquidity through IPOs (initial public offerings). While an IPO is not technically a liquidity event (it is actually another investment event), it can provide liquidity to shareholders. After a holding or lock-up period specified by the SEC or other regulatory body of 90 to 180 days, existing investors may choose to sell some or all of their holdings. (A liquidity event is not to be confused with the liquidation of a company. In a liquidation event the company's business is discontinued and assets are sold to pay off the company's debts and then pay off shareholders with any remaining capital.)

A successful exit or liquidity event for an investor is one in which the value of their shares in your company increases substantially from the time they invested in your company to the time they convert to cash. Not every company will reach a large liquidity event. In fact, 90% of all startups will not only fail to reach a liquidity event (*http://on.mash.to/2ccSAqk*), but will go out of business entirely.

Why Do So Many Startups Fail?

The Startup Genome Project (*http://bit.ly/2cL5EBE*), which analyzed more than 3,200 startups, found that more than 90% of startups fail due primarily to self-destruction rather than competition. It also reported that for the 10% of startups that do succeed, most encounter several near-death experiences along the way. The biggest reason for failure reported in the study was *premature scaling*, which affected 74% of startups.

Premature scaling is defined in the Startup Genome report as spending money beyond the essentials on growing the business. Essentially this means spending money on hiring, marketing, operations, and other growth before achieving *product/market fit*—a term first coined by Marc Andreessen of Andreessen Horowitz to describe a startup in a good market with a product that can satisfy that market. To avoid premature scaling a company must first achieve product/market fit, and then invest in growth. In other words: nail it, then scale it.

A recent study by CrunchBase (*http://bit.ly/2cGYmQx*), a database of the startup ecosystem operated by TechCrunch, listed other contributing factors to startup failure, including a lack of market need, running out of cash, not having the right team, getting outcompeted, cost issues, poor product, and lack of business model.

Businesses that attract venture capital must have the potential to provide returns much higher than the stock market. Why? Because investing in a startup has much higher risk than investing in the stock market. Your company doesn't just need to have the potential to generate a slightly higher return than the single-digit average returns on the stock market. It needs to have the potential to provide investors a return so substantial that it can make up for any losses in their portfolios. A rule of thumb is that early-stage venture capital investors are seeking from 3 to 10 times return on investment. Later-stage investors, investing later in a company's lifecycle and taking on less risk, target lower returns.

A recent study from the Kauffman Foundation (*http://bit.ly/ 2cXAV7S*), the largest American foundation to focus on entrepreneurship, reported on average returns from a diversified portfolio of 10 or more companies. The report found that on average, half of the companies in an investor's portfolio will fail (returning nothing or less than the capital invested). Another 3 or 4 will provide a modest return on investment of 1 to 5 times the principal invested—known as a *cash-on-cash return*—and 1 or hopefully 2 of the 10 companies will return 10 to 30 times on the initial investment over a 5- to 8-year period.

By seeking high returns on the winners in its portfolio, an investor hopes to make up for its losses, targeting a 3x return on investment overall. Companies capable of contributing to these types of returns must be able to rapidly scale into very large businesses, and they need to be addressing a very large market. When you take venture capital into your company, it is your responsibility to provide the highest return possible for your investors. If your intention as an entrepreneur is not to build a massive, fast-growth company, your interests will not be aligned with those of early-stage investors.

The Unicorn

Before we dive into what investors are looking for in fundable companies, let's set the stage by talking about the most coveted investment outcome —the unicorn. A unicorn is a company that has reached a $1 billion or higher valuation either in the public market or during a private investment round. The term was coined by Aileen Lee, founder of Cowboy Ventures.

The most talked about, and highest valued, unicorn today is Uber. Uber is a mobile app that allows users to request a taxi or an Uber driver who uses their own car to pick the user up. Uber has a valuation of $62.5 billion based on its December 2015 fundraising round (*http://bloom.bg/ 2cq3iJ5*), led by venture capital firms like Lowercase Capital, Benchmark Capital, and Google Ventures.

Investors dream of being an early investor in the next unicorn. For some investors it is for prestige, while for others (especially venture capital funds larger than $150 million), it's not a matter of preference but of necessity (*http://bit.ly/2c8NzRC*). In order to provide an adequate return to their investors, larger funds usually need a share in at least one company of a $1 billion-plus valuation. This means that larger investment funds will not invest in a company if they don't believe it has the potential to become a unicorn, or if they believe the founder doesn't have the ambition to build a billion-dollar business.

If your market is not large enough to support a unicorn, or your business model will never scale to create a billion-dollar company, you can still be fundable—but you won't be able to raise your funding from a larger venture capital fund (more than $150 million in capital).

There are many great businesses that will never become unicorns, and many entrepreneurs who do not aspire to build unicorns. Very early-stage investors can still make significant profits by investing in companies that never become unicorns.

Dave McClure, founding partner at 500 Startups, has coined terms for successful companies that haven't joined what has been called "the unicorn club." Dave refers to companies that have a valuation of more than $100 million as "centaurs" and startups that have a valuation of more than $10 million as "ponies."

Early investors can make a lot of money off of centaurs and ponies, and even off of companies with valuations lower than $10 million.

Investor Expectations as You Grow

While the ability to provide an adequate return is one way to broadly define what makes a company fundable, investors' expectations of your company will vary depending on the stage it's in. How investors evaluate your company at the early stage, when you're raising your first round, will be different from how you are evaluated at later stages.

A company's first round is commonly referred to as its *seed round*. This is the earliest, and often the smallest, round a company will raise. Between 2010 and 2014, the average seed round in the US was generally between $0.36 million and $1.5 million (*http://bit.ly/2cGZ3cy*). The size of your seed round will be determined by how much money you need to reach your next milestone. This amount varies depending on your product, the barriers to entry in your market, and your geography.

Following a seed round is a *Series A*. The average Series A deal in the US is between $2 million and $7 million. Series A financing goes to companies that have been able to prove out a reliable sales model. Money raised in a Series A is generally used to prove that the company's customer acquisition strategies can perform at scale.

After Series A financing, companies can continue to raise capital throughout their lifetimes. Each round typically receives a new letter: Series B, Series C, Series D, and so on. Capital raised in later-stage rounds is invested in further growth. At this point the business, while still risky, is much lower risk than a seed-stage company, with a comparably lower return profile.

Because companies at different stages are evaluated differently, what round a company says it is raising sets the tone of the conversation with investors.

Founders will sometimes characterize a funding round as being earlier than it actually is because they believe this will lower the investor's expectations of their product, traction, and growth. For example, a founder will say the company is raising a seed round when it is really an A round. This may lower an investor's expectations, as an earlier funding round suggests that the company has raised less money and has been in business for a shorter period of time.

That said, sometimes founders get a bit carried away, raising multiple seed rounds so that they don't have to say they are raising a Series A. Likewise, companies raising a B round might say they are raising an A, also to lower investor expectations. The best investors aren't fooled; they can look at the company and the amount of time and capital that have gone into it and determine what round it is actually raising—regardless of what the founders might call it.

Figure 1-1 shows a tweet by Marc Andreessen on this topic.

Marc Andreessen ✓
@pmarca

Cautionary note: No competent VC is actually fooled when you show up after raising $6M in seed financing and say you're now raising an A!

RETWEETS LIKES
97   161

9:30 PM - 6 Oct 2014

FIGURE 1-1. The best investors can tell what round a company is actually raising

Tier 1 Venture Funds

The highest-caliber venture funds are referred to as Tier 1 venture funds. These funds tend to be larger and participate mostly in Series A+ rounds. There is no set ranking of VCs, and tiers are more a matter of opinion, but funds commonly referred to in the industry as Tier 1 include Andreessen Horowitz, Sequoia Capital, Accel Partners, and Benchmark Capital. The following are some of the factors that play into a firm being considered Tier 1:

Brand value
   Whether a VC firm adds legitimacy to the companies it invests in. Will it raise the profile of those companies? Does the firm have a strong track record of success?

Returns
   The amount a fund has historically made back on its investments and the consistency with which it delivers good returns to its investors.

Network
   How connected the firm is and what introductions it will be able to make to open doors for its companies.

Other added value
   Other ways that venture firms help their companies with things like sales, recruiting, or finding exit opportunities.

If you are able to raise from Tier 1s, meaning you have the connections and the business fundamentals to attract their interest, they are who you want to raise from. That said, as appealing as Tier 1s may be, if you don't have the right connections and aren't a hot deal, you may waste time courting Tier 1s and should look at putting more effort into conversations with lower-tier investors.

> **TIP** Sand Hill Road is a street in Menlo Park, California, that has the largest concentration of VCs in the world (*http://bloom.bg/2cjPYds*). Almost every prominent company in Silicon Valley has received funding from at least one investor on Sand Hill Road. Kleiner Perkins Caufield & Byers was the first VC to set up shop on Sand Hill Road, in 1972. Sand Hill Road also boasts the most expensive office space in the United States, at $141 per square foot (*http://cnb.cx/2clBe8H*).

Conclusion

This chapter has introduced what it means to be venture capital fundable. Understanding how investors make money, why some startups fail, and the holy grail of venture capital—the unicorn—will help you communicate with investors on their terms.

The remainder of the book will focus in detail on investor expectations for seed-stage companies in particular. We will take a deep dive into how investors discover, evaluate, and invest in these opportunities, and how you can position your company to secure their investment.

Even if your business is not a perfect match for venture funding today, based on what we've discussed in this chapter and what we'll cover throughout the rest of the book, don't worry: you'll be able to continue to use the knowledge you'll gain in this book to become a fundable opportunity.

You will also have the opportunity to reach your goals through other forms of capital that may be better suited to your business. In the next chapter we'll dive into each of these alternatives as we weigh the pros and cons of venture capital.

CHAPTER 2

Venture Capital: The Pros, Cons, and Alternatives

TODAY, VENTURE FINANCING IS GLAMORIZED BY THE MEDIA. IT'S LIKE A scorecard for founders and entrepreneurs to compare how they are doing relative to their peers.

Financing announcements on TechCrunch, movies like *The Social Network*, and HBO's hit show *Silicon Valley* have led many founders to believe that venture capital is the natural next step for any budding startup. It's true that venture capital can be a great way to finance growth, and that the right investors can add a stamp of legitimacy and provide valuable connections to further your business. But venture capital isn't right for every founder or every company.

As mentioned in Chapter 1, less than 25% of all businesses actually receive venture capital, either through angel investments (24%) or venture capital firms (1%). The other 75% of businesses turn to other strategies and forms of capital to finance their growth.

It's not just small companies that don't raise venture capital. There are many large companies that either didn't raise any venture capital at all, or were already fairly well established before fundraising.

When Dell raised its first venture capital financing, it already had $60 million in revenue. eBay had over $4.5 million in revenue before Benchmark Capital invested in the company. Oracle's first product was funded by a government contract, and Cisco already had $5 million in revenue before Sequoia invested. These companies were able to establish themselves without seed venture capital.

Taking on venture capital will have a substantial impact on the course of your company, whether it be from friends and family (angel investors) or professional investors (venture capitalists). Many founders rush into seeking venture capital financing without fully understanding what they are getting themselves into. In this chapter we will discuss the pros and cons of venture capital financing and introduce the five most common alternatives to venture capital.

Arguments in Favor of Venture Capital

First, let's discuss the reasons why venture capital can be an attractive funding option for your startup.

ACCELERATED GROWTH

Venture capital allows for accelerated growth. It allows you to build faster, expand to new markets, compete with industry incumbents (which often have more money to invest in product and marketing), and move faster than other startups entering the market with less funding.

NETWORK

Great venture capital investors can provide valuable advice, expertise, guidance, and connections to the companies they invest in. By giving investors an equity stage in the business, you are building a long-term support network that you can tap into over time.

CREDIBILITY

Raising venture capital in today's startup world is seen as a badge of honor, for better or for worse. Getting well-respected investors to buy into your business can be a way of building credibility. This credibility makes it easier to attract media attention, secure new customers, and recruit talent.

EXPOSURE

Raising venture capital is seen as a significant milestone in the startup world and is often newsworthy. Closing a venture round can get you into some of the top tech media outlets, get you on stage at industry conferences, and put you on the radar of industry leaders. If your business could benefit from exposure of this type, announcing a venture capital round can be a great way to get it.

BENCHMARKING

Valuations of early-stage, high-growth, and pre-revenue companies are a bit more art than science, even during liquidity events like an acquisition. Let's imagine a pre-revenue company that has never raised venture capital is in acquisition talks—how will its valuation be determined? It will likely be some combination of market rate for similar companies, what the acquiring company is willing to pay, and what the entrepreneurs are willing to sell for. Now let's imagine that company just raised venture capital at a $10 million valuation. All of a sudden the value of the company is tied to that number. Unless it's a fire sale, the company is very unlikely to take an offer below that valuation because its investors would lose money. For early-stage companies this benchmark can often help the entrepreneur get more in the event of a sale; however, if an equity financing round was done at a low valuation, it may actually serve as a negative.

FUNDING RESEARCH AND DEVELOPMENT

Sometimes there is a lot of upfront research and development (R&D) required to launch a product (examples are virtual reality software or satellite technology products). When a lot of R&D is required, significant capital investment is also required to fund the period of time prelaunch when the company is not generating revenue. Venture capital is a popular way to fund this type of project, as it can be high risk/high reward, and few other forms of capital are willing to risk such early-stage investment.

Arguments Against Venture Capital

Now that we have covered the arguments in favor of funding your company through venture capital, let's take a look at the downside of venture capital and some of the risks it may pose to you and your business.

LOSS OF EQUITY AND CONTROL

When you take venture capital you are selling a piece of your company. That means that in a future liquidity event, you'll have a smaller piece of the pie. In addition to giving away a piece of your company, you will often be required to give some level of control to your investors as part of the venture capital process. That may take the form of giving up a board seat to your investors and could mean giving your investors the right to reject future funding rounds or acquisition offers.

Many entrepreneurs start their businesses because they want freedom. But as the CEO of a venture-backed business, you'll need to be able to manage the interests of multiple stakeholders. Unlike banks, equity investors tend to provide more than just capital. They provide guidance and connections and will often have an active interest in your operations.

DISTRACTION

Raising venture capital takes time—time that could be spent building your business. Ask any entrepreneur who has raised venture capital, and they will tell you that for the period of time that they were fundraising it was their full-time job, and often the company's core metrics take a hit because of it. In some cases six months spent building product or getting sales revenue would be a better use of time than fundraising.

CHANGED EXIT OPPORTUNITIES

Raising money changes your potential exit strategy. First of all, raising money will likely push you toward an exit. VC investors are looking to see a return within 5–10 years so that they can provide returns to the funds' investors. Secondly, raising money will make it hard for you to accept acquisition offers that might have been in your interest prefinancing. Let's say your company, which raised money at a $30 million valuation, gets an offer for $10 million. Your investors have no liquidation preference, meaning they have no right to get their money out ahead of other shareholders and you as the entrepreneur, who own 40% of the company. In this scenario, you may look at the $10 million offer and think $4 million for you personally looks pretty good. But assuming your investors have blocking rights on a sale, they will reject the offer, not wanting to take a loss on their investment.

Avoid a False Sense of Success

Many entrepreneurs fall into the trap of seeing raising money as business success. Companies that have raised large funding rounds are seen as heroes, and the media can't get enough of them. But the truth is that raising money is not success. Just because a company has raised funding does not mean that it has built a strong business or reached any concrete milestone. When entrepreneurs who have raised money drink the Kool-Aid of today's startup culture, they may conflate having raised money with being a successful business, leading them to make bad decisions like prematurely scaling, overspending, or spending more time being socialites than on building their companies.

Five Alternatives to Venture Capital

We've weighed the pros and cons, but it's still too early to decide whether venture capital is the right decision for your business—first we must look at your alternatives.

Unlike venture capital, the alternatives covered here are nondilutive. An average equity round of financing results in founders giving up 10–30% ownership of the company, while alternative forms of financing can allow you to keep full ownership and still raise the money you require for growth.

However, every form of financing, dilutive or not, has its pros and cons. We will cover the five most common alternatives to venture capital here.

If you decide not to raise venture capital, the alternatives covered in this chapter could become your primary sources of capital. If you do decide to raise venture capital, understanding the other sources of financing available to early-stage companies will give you a sense of your BATNA (Best Alternative to a Negotiated Agreement) and an understanding of additional ways to capitalize your business.

REWARD-BASED CROWDFUNDING

Crowdfunding is the practice of funding a project or venture by raising monetary contributions from a large number of people. Reward-based crowdfunding is when contributors pay money to back a product or project and expect to receive a reward, oftentimes the product itself, if the crowdfunding campaign is successful.

Reward-based crowdfunding has grown dramatically in popularity over the past few years as a means of both proving demand for a product and financing initial production, with the most popular crowdfunding platforms being Kickstarter and Indiegogo.

Equity Crowdfunding

Equity-based crowdfunding is different from reward-based crowdfunding. It is another form of crowdfunding whereby contributors invest money into a company and receive equity rather than a reward in exchange for their money. Unlike reward-based crowdfunding, equity crowdfunding isn't an alternative to venture capital; it's just a specific form of venture financing.

Equity crowdfunding has recently risen in popularity as a tool for early-stage entrepreneurs trying to raise money, and both private investors and venture capitalists have been known to invest on equity crowdfunding platforms like AngelList, FundersClub, and SeedInvest, among others.

Why crowdfund?

Crowdfunding has emerged outside of the traditional financial system. Reward-based crowdfunding allows entrepreneurs to maintain full ownership and control of their companies, and the money invested does not have to be repaid.

For companies looking to produce a physical product, reward-based crowdfunding has proven to be an incredibly powerful financing platform, with some products—like the Pebble watch and the Ouya gaming console—raising over $10 million through crowdfunding.

Crowdfunding can be used as an alternative to venture capital, as a marketing tactic after venture capital is raised, or as a way to get the attention of venture capital investors. By proving the demand for your product on a crowdfunding platform, you can prove to investors that there is a market need.

What is the downside?

While there are many upsides to reward-based crowdfunding, there are also some risks. First, reward-based crowdfunding hasn't yet proven to be a reliable form of financing for software- or service-based companies, so it's not right for every business. Secondly, crowdfunding, like raising venture capital, is very time-consuming. Running a successful crowdfunding campaign requires intense planning and attention to detail. Crowdfunding can be a full-time job leading up to and during a campaign and can take you and your team away from building other parts of your business. Finally, unlike with venture capital funds, you need to provide something in exchange for the money. Delivering on your crowdfunding promises can be extremely costly and time-consuming, and this is something most entrepreneurs greatly underestimate before they begin.

COMMERCIAL LOANS

A commercial loan is a debt-based funding arrangement that a business can set up with a financial institution. Much like venture capital, commercial loans are often used by corporations to fund large capital expenditures that a business may otherwise be unable to afford.

Why commercial loans?

Commercial loans are a more traditional form of financing, often provided by banks. They generally require that a company already have revenue in order to qualify, and they are sometimes secured against company assets. Commercial loans allow companies to avoid any loss of equity or control and can be faster to secure than venture capital. Financial institutions providing commercial loans are not buying into your business, so they will not actively interfere with your operations.

What is the downside?

Commercial loans are often neither accessible nor particularly well suited to early-stage ventures. Pre-revenue companies without significant assets will find it very difficult to secure traditional commercial loans. When a young company does manage to secure a commercial loan, it is often required to provide personal guarantees, meaning if the company isn't able to pay back the debt the entrepreneur will be on the hook for the money personally.

Beyond just the personal financial risk they may impose, commercial loans may simply not be a practical way to finance a company that expects to be pre-revenue or cash flow negative for a long period of time. When a company is unable to pay off its debts, those debts will sit as a liability on the company's books. A company with many liabilities is less attractive to acquirers, and will be forced to use future revenues to pay off those debts rather than invest in growth.

Venture Debt

Venture debt is a complement to equity financing. It provides flexibility and can be less costly when structured properly. Unlike a commercial loan, venture debt is specifically designed for startups and growth companies that do not have positive cash flows or significant assets to use as collateral. Venture debt, which can sometimes be secured against a company's accounts receivable, can be used to make infrastructure purchases or may simply be used to finance growth in the place of an equity round. Financial institutions and individuals offering venture debt as a substitute for equity financing tend to follow a similar opportunity assessment process as they would if they were investing in an equity round. Venture debt is typically structured as a loan or series of loans with warrants for company stock to compensate for the higher risk of the investment. Many venture debt shops will want warrant coverage in the amount of 5–20% of the loan value.

GOVERNMENT GRANTS

A government grant is a financial award given by federal, regional, or local governments to eligible grantees. It is not expected to be repaid by the recipient. Government grants for small businesses—especially those addressing social problems, those developing new technologies, or those with minority founders—can be found in most regions.

Why grants?

Grants are a great form of financing in that they essentially provide you with free money. No equity needs to be given up and the money never has to be repaid. Grants are also helpful for companies that are not yet appealing opportunities to venture capital investors. Grants are generally awarded based on specific criteria very different from the criteria of venture capitalists—for example, revenue and growth may not be as important to the government as social impact or research. The funds a company secures through grant funding can be invested in product and sales to get the company to a state at which it is venture fundable.

What is the downside?

Grants generally come hand in hand with a long application process and strict reporting requirements. While it is marketed as free money, the truth is that companies need to work very hard to get grant funding.

Applicants often write essays, build business plans, and draft proposals simply to be considered. And once accepted, they often need to keep meticulous records of their progress to remain in good standing or to get the next installment of the grant. This is often work the company would never have done were it not applying for the grant, and it is a distraction from the company's core business.

Grants are also quite unpredictable. What grants are available for what industries varies greatly over time and region to region. Grant funding may not be available to your business. Who will get a grant, and when they will receive the money, is also sometimes quite hard to predict, making it a risky financing source to rely on.

GOVERNMENT SUBSIDIES AND TAX INCENTIVES

A tax incentive is a reduction in a company's taxable income or return on taxes paid by a company based on a number of possible factors. For example, if a government is looking to encourage growth in a particular sector (such as technology), it may offer tax incentives to companies working in that industry. A subsidy is a monetary allowance paid by the government for a specific purpose. The types of government subsidies available to a company can vary greatly depending on the industry or region.

Why government subsidies and tax incentives?

Subsidies and tax incentives are ways of financing a business that don't require a company to give up any equity or control. They tend to be much more predictable than government grants, being given out to more companies and requiring shorter application processes, if any application process at all. This form of financing can sometimes be so substantial that it affects a company's decision on where to locate its operations—which is often what the government intended.

Regions that don't typically attract startup activity tend to have more aggressive government incentive programs, as an attempt to make up for other shortcomings in the startup ecosystem. For example, Silicon Valley may not need as many government incentives to attract companies as other regions in the US due to its mature startup ecosystem.

Canada is a great example of a region that uses government incentives to attract startups, via its popular tax incentive program called the Scientific Research and Experimental Development program, or SR&ED for short.

Most high-tech startups operating in Canada qualify for the program, which provides support in the form of tax credits and refunds to companies that conduct scientific research or experimental development in Canada. Depending on the province in which the business is located, companies can recover up to 64% of qualifying expenditures, such as salaries, contractor fees, and materials spent on research and development.

For many startups that means hundreds of thousands, and sometimes millions, of dollars back from the government each year. This program has been a large contributor to Canadian companies maintaining their operations in Canada while they grow and has even attracted many international firms that have set up operations in the country.

What is the downside?

Government subsidies and tax incentives are not always an option, depending on your region or industry. These programs can also encourage behavior not in the interest of the company. While it may be cheaper to operate in a region offering these incentives, perhaps the company would have been better off operating in a more expensive environment with a more developed startup ecosystem and support network. Specific requirements of these programs may also encourage you to run projects that you would not have otherwise run, were it not for the funding.

BOOTSTRAPPING

You've probably heard people refer to "bootstrapped" startups before. Bootstrapping is when an entrepreneur starts a company with little capital and attempts to found and build it entirely from personal finances or from its operating revenues.

Why bootstrapping?

Bootstrapping is a great way for you to maintain full control and ownership of your company as you grow. That means that in the event of a sale, you as the entrepreneur will get a larger piece of the pie. Bootstrapping encourages strong business fundamentals. We are rarely as careful with other people's money as we are with our own. When a company needs to live off its own revenues, it tends to prioritize initiatives that make money and operate more efficiently.

What is the downside?

Bootstrapping is not the best decision for every startup. It is particularly effective in businesses where there is low competition, and no need to rapidly expand in order to protect against competitors taking ownership of new markets. But bootstrapping is often not a viable strategy in winner-take-all markets, land grabs, or businesses where there are network effects, meaning every additional user creates more value for other users. Without the funds to invest in product or expand rapidly, a company may lose out to better-funded competitors who are able to establish themselves faster. Bootstrapping may also lead a company to prioritize short-term gains over long-term value. The company may take on service contracts that pay the bills this month (but are gone the next month), or avoid high-risk or research-driven projects that don't have an immediate impact on the bottom line. Finally, bootstrapping is not always an option; there are some businesses with large enough startup or infrastructure costs that they simply wouldn't be possible without outside capital.

Conclusion

In this chapter we've covered the pros and cons of venture capital and five alternative forms of financing. While venture capital comes with risks and rewards, you can see that every form of financing comes with its own list of pros and cons. There is no silver bullet, and you will likely end up utilizing many different forms of financing throughout the lifecycle of your company. As an entrepreneur setting out to finance your growth, it's important to understand your unique market and your needs in order to come up with the right mix of funding for you.

Exercise: Weighing the Pros and Cons

Throughout the book we've included exercises to help you prepare for your funding round. In your first exercise you will be evaluating the pros and cons of venture financing for your business and rating the viability of other funding methods.

Complete the following exercise and then reflect on your learnings. To raise money, you need a venture-backable business (you need to be fundable). You also need to be willing to accept the downsides that come with venture funding, and you should have carefully rated the likelihood of achieving your business objectives through other funding means.

If after completing this exercise you determine that either your business does not meet the criteria of a fundable startup or you aren't willing to accept the implications of taking on venture capital, rest assured that it doesn't mean you can't make a lot of money running your business. I encourage you to continue reading, as all founders—not just those actively raising money today—will be able to get value from the lessons on growth, sales, and strategy taught throughout this book.

Are You a Venture-Backable Business?

Did you have an initial product or prototype?	Yes [ ]	No [ ]
Have you proven market demand?	Yes [ ]	No [ ]
Does your company have at least 10% month-over-month growth potential on your most important success metric (i.e., revenue or daily active users)?	Yes [ ]	No [ ]
Do you plan to provide a liquidity event within 5–10 years?	Yes [ ]	No [ ]

Are You OK with the Downsides of Venture Capital?

Loss of equity and control	Yes [ ]	No [ ]
Distraction	Yes [ ]	No [ ]
Limited exit opportunities	Yes [ ]	No [ ]

Rate Your Alternatives

How strong a fit would you consider each of the following funding alternatives for your business, on a scale from 1 to 5, with 5 being the strongest fit?

Reward-based crowdfunding	1	2	3	4	5
Commercial loans	1	2	3	4	5
Government grants	1	2	3	4	5
Government subsidies and tax incentives	1	2	3	4	5
Bootstrapping	1	2	3	4	5
Would you be able to reach your business objectives without the added capital venture funding would provide?	Yes [ ]		No [ ]		

Based on your answers, take a minute to reflect on whether venture funding is the right decision for your business today.

_____

_____

CHAPTER 3

Ownership and Valuations

Now that we've covered the basic principles of venture capital, it's time to dive deeper into its mechanics.

Often entrepreneurs are intimidated by venture financing because of the intricacies of structuring a funding round. But the truth is that the mechanics of venture capital are actually quite straightforward: investors put money into your company in exchange for a percentage of ownership, or in some cases in exchange for debt.

This chapter will introduce you to how funding rounds actually work and arm you with the knowledge and confidence to hit the fundraising trail. We will cover ownership, how it's calculated, and how it changes over time, and we will discuss different options you have when structuring a funding round.

Understanding Ownership

You know your company meets the criteria of a venture-fundable business and you've reviewed the risks and rewards of venture capital funding, but there is one important piece to understand before you decide that venture capital is right for you: ownership. As an entrepreneur you need to understand how it gets divided up, how it can change over time, and why it matters.

Company ownership is measured in terms of shares. Every company can have a different total number of shares, which is immaterial to the calculation of ownership. Shares get divided up among a company's owners based on their percentage ownership, and this list of owners is known as a company's *shareholders*.

The document used to communicate a company's ownership structure is called a *capitalization table* or *cap table*. The cap table takes the form of a spreadsheet or table listing all the major shareholders and their proportional, or *pro rata*, ownership of all shares issued by the company. The table is the easiest way to ascertain a company's overall capital structure at a glance.

Getting Your Cap Table

While it is certainly possible to create your own cap table, my recommendation would be that you request a copy from your lawyer.

If you don't yet have a lawyer, or aren't yet incorporated, your first order of business should be to find a reliable corporate lawyer to help you through your funding round. You don't just want to work with any lawyer; you should work with one that has experience in early-stage startup funding, as investors will very quickly get frustrated by a novice lawyer unfamiliar with market terms and best practices. Luckily, many startup lawyers have very reasonable starting rates for prefunding companies, and others will defer their fees entirely until you raise your first round of capital. Talk to other founders who have raised capital, and look for an introduction to legal counsel that they would recommend.

Template: The Funded Cap Table Template

Looking to create your own cap table? The Funded Cap Table Template will help you map out your company's ownership structure. (Alternatively, rather than creating your own cap table by hand using a template, you can use cap table management software like Capshare or Sharewave.)

Download the Funded Cap Table Template at *TheEntrepreneursGuide.com*.

In addition to ownership, a cap table will list the various prices paid by these stakeholders for their stakes. When shares of the company are sold, they should be sold at fair market value (this helps to avoid negative tax consequences). As a result, it is common for founders who are issued shares in their company at incorporation to have a purchase price set at a nominal amount because the company is arguably not worth anything at that time (i.e., it has no operating history, little to no assets, and thus little value).

This value will change—hopefully increase—as the company matures, and new shareholders will need to buy their stakes in the company for a higher price.

As new shares are sold throughout the lifetime of the company, the ownership held by each original shareholder on the cap table will decrease on a pro rata basis, based on the percentage of the company sold. This is known as *dilution*.

While dilution may not feel great, bringing on new investors can be an important part of helping your company to grow quickly, thus increasing the value of your stake in the company overall. As the common adage goes, you're getting a smaller piece of a bigger pie.

Share Classes

On a cap table there are different classes of equities listed, most notably common shares, preferred shares, and stock options. Share class can have a significant effect on how shares perform at different events in a company's lifecycle. Here, we will go through each share class, who typically owns shares of that class, and the special properties of that share class.

COMMON SHARES

As an entrepreneur, you hold common shares. Holders of common stock exercise control by electing a board of directors and voting on corporate policy; however, common shares are at the bottom of the priority ladder for ownership structure when it comes to liquidity. In the case of a liquidity event, common shareholders have rights to a company's assets only after all other classes of shareholders have been paid in full.

PREFERRED SHARES

Preferred shares are what will generally be held by your venture capital investors. These shareholders do not have the same voting privileges as holders of common shares; however, preferred shares do carry certain advantages. These privileges get negotiated at the time of a funding round, and the shareholders' agreement gets altered to reflect these changes. We will cover some of the finer points of negotiation in future chapters, but in general the main benefit of preferred shares is that their holders take priority over common shareholders when it comes time to pay dividends or in the case of a liquidity event. Most preferred share-holders also have both voting rights and veto rights. A veto right is often more important. Veto rights and protective provisions include things like restricting the company's ability to issue new shares, raise debt, or hire founders' family members or spouses without permission. They may also restrict payment of dividends without permission, changes to compensation and equity grants without permission, or mergers/acquisitions without permission. If you raise multiple funding rounds, the preferences of these shares get stacked in order of priority, with the highest level of priority going to the most recent investors—this is typically referred to as "last in, first out."

STOCK OPTIONS

A stock option is a privilege, sold by your startup, giving buyers the right (but not the obligation) to buy stock at an agreed-upon price within a certain period or on a specific date. Stock options are a key part of employee compensation for startups, helping to make up for the added risk taken on by employees and the fact that they often receive below-market wages. Stock options also help to align early employees at a company with the interests of shareholders. As the company increases in value, so does the value of an employee's stock options.

How Stock Options Work

Stock options don't behave like typical shares. To help you understand how stock options affect you and your funding round, let's walk through the mechanics of how they actually work.

When employees are given stock options, they are given the option to buy a certain number of shares at a set price, known as the *strike price*. This option is granted through an Employee Stock Option Plan, or ESOP. Options vest over a period of time while the employee is employed, usually annually over four years. The vesting period is the time that an employee must wait in order to be able to exercise their option.

Exercising an option means that the employee notifies the company that they would like to buy the stock at the strike price on their option plan. Once employees purchase their stock options, they become shareholders in the company and benefit from increases in company valuation—much like you, the entrepreneur. The more the individual shares increase in value from the strike price to the price at which the option holder ultimately sells their shares during a liquidity event, the more money the employee stands to make. This increase in value is known as the *spread*.

Simply knowing the number of shares and the prices at which ESOPs are granted won't tell you very much about their value. In order to make sense out of options, you need to understand what percentage of the company those options represent.

If there are 1,000,000 shares outstanding, and an employee is granted 1,000 options at $1 and decides to exercise those options, they will pay $1,000 and own 1,000 shares, or 0.1% of the company. If the company sells for anything above $1,000,000, the employee will profit from the options.

However, if there are instead 10 million shares outstanding, and an employee is granted 1,000 options at $1, and decides to exercise those options, they will pay $1,000 and own 1,000 shares, but this time it's only 0.01% of the company. In this case the company would need to sell for $10,000,000 for the employee to profit from the options.

As mentioned earlier in this chapter, companies don't have a standard number of shares, so when evaluating the value of a stock option plan, asking for the number of outstanding shares can be important.

There is no set rule as to what percentage of the company each early employee should be granted as options. But here are some guidelines that Venture Hacks has published (*http://bit.ly/2cClEJe*) relating to equity shares for nonfounding new hires in particular roles, based on Silicon Valley standards:

- CEO: 5–10%

- COO: 2–5%

- A VP: 1–2%

- A lead engineer: 0.5–1%

- An engineer with 5+ years' experience: 0.33–0.66%

- A manager or junior engineer: 0.2–0.33%

Option Pools

Shares set aside to be granted to employees as stock options are listed on the company's cap table. This is known as the *option pool*. The average option pool is 10% per round of financing, with exceptional cases being 5% or 15%. Employees who get into the startup early will usually receive a greater percentage of the option pool than employees who arrive later. When added to the cap table, this option pool dilutes all other shareholders on a pro rata basis depending on the size of the pool.

If an option pool does not already exist, one is generally carved out when the company is raising money because investors don't want to share in the dilution after they become shareholders. You want to negotiate for a smaller option pool, because it decreases your dilution. Negotiation over option pool size is really just a negotiation around price, with investors seeing larger option pools as a way to protect themselves from future dilution by stretching out the time before a new option pool needs to be created.

If stock options in an option pool are not granted or exercised, the shares are redistributed on a pro rata basis to all shareholders. In fact, you can create a shareholder provision that unissued options will be returned to the founders and angels, as opposed to institutional investors—a bonus for you on exit! If a Series A or later investor objects to the provision and insists on distribution to all shareholders, it becomes a noncritical negotiation point you can agree to. You may find agreeing to this requirement makes the new investor more lenient in other matters.

A slightly different approach is to set up a fixed-percentage option pool. So, for example, an option pool could be specified as being 10% of the company no matter how much investment is brought in.

Building a Hiring Plan

You can often justify a smaller option pool by creating a corresponding hiring plan for the next 18 months, showing that your option pool will cover your upcoming hiring needs.

The advantages here are that every investor knows in advance what the dilution will be, no subsequent negotiations are required regarding the size of the pool, and there should always be sufficient stock available to employees and others no matter how large the company becomes.

Template: The Funded Hiring Plan Template

You can use the Funded Hiring Plan Template to plan your next hires and esti-mate their stock option compensations. Having a hiring plan will help you jus-tify a specific option pool size at the time of financing.

Download the Funded Hiring Plan Template at *TheEntrepreneurs-Guide.com.*

WARRANTS

Warrants are similar to stock options in that they are a contractual right to purchase shares at a particular price, for a particular period of time. How-ever, warrants are different in that they are generally granted as part of an investment transaction, unlike options, which are generally granted as compensation to employees or contractors. Thus, warrants do not have the vesting and are generally applied to the most recent share class as opposed to common shares.

Calculating Valuations

The price at which shares are purchased is referred to as the *pre-money valuation.* The *post-money valuation* of a company is the pre-money value plus the total amount of new capital brought into the company through the recent sale.

A common rule of thumb is that investors want 10–30% equity per round. The more leverage you (the entrepreneur) have, the higher the percentage of the company you can keep, and thus the lower the valua-tion.

Let's look at an example. Assume you raise a $1.5 million seed round. The investors have asked for 10% of the company in exchange for this investment.

This indicates that the company and its investors agreed to a $13.5 million pre-money investment valuation. The company's value will increase by the amount of the investment, and the post-money valuation will be $13.5 million + $1.5 million for a total of $15 million.

The value of the business before the investment is known as the pre-money valuation, and the value of the business after the investment is known as the post-money valuation.

Now let's take that same example and assume the investors get 20% for their $1.5 million investment, double the stake they received for the same amount of money in the last example. In this case, $1.5 million for 20% indicates a $6 million pre-money valuation and a $7.5 million post-money valuation, half the valuation of our last example.

While we will not be going into detail about later-stage funding in this book, it is important to know that your first round of funding is likely not your last—particularly if you are successful and go on to build a very large business. You'll want to make sure that the valuation you set in a funding round is neither too high nor too low.

Too low a valuation could give your investors such a large share in the company that there is no room for other investors in future rounds without diluting you so much that you are no longer motivated to run the business. Too high a valuation could set the standard so high that you aren't able to match the valuation in future funding rounds, resulting in a *down round*—where the company raises at a valuation lower than its last round. Down rounds are very bad signaling and can be very punitive in terms of dilution to common stockholders.

Down rounds are demoralizing for a startup and pose a risk to its reputation. They are equally frustrating to investors because a down round allows later-stage investors to pay less per share than angels and early-stage investors. It also means that the startup needs to give up more equity to secure funding. This means that dilution for existing shareholders is much greater than it would be during a round where the company's valuation increased.

Factors Affecting Valuation

In today's market typical valuations for early-stage companies in North America range from $1 million to $7 million, with the average seed round taking place at a valuation between $3 million and $5 million. Next we'll cover the four primary factors that play into a company's valuation.

MARKET INTEREST

The number of interested investors at the table looking to invest in your company will affect the price. Many interested investors will drive the price up, allowing you to play offers off of one another. Few investors interested in the deal will result in a lower valuation if the investors know you don't have any other options.

EXPERIENCE

Your experience level as an entrepreneur will factor into the price of the round. More experienced entrepreneurs, especially those that have made money for investors in the past, can command a premium.

LOCATION

Valuations in startup hubs tend to be higher than in smaller markets. The highest valuations today can be seen in San Francisco, New York, London, and Tel Aviv. If you are not in a startup hub, you likely won't need to raise as much money and won't have as much competition from investors, driving your valuation down.

COMPANY STAGE

The more mature your product, and the more revenue you are bringing in, the more appealing your investment will be and the higher the valuation can be.

TIP AngelList Valuation Tool

If you would like to see market valuations for companies in various geographies or sectors, check out AngelList's valuation tool (*https://angel.co/valuations*). AngelList is an online directory of early-stage investors and startups and an equity crowdfunding platform. It is used by many startups as a place to market a funding round. The AngelList valuation tool exposes average valuations taken from deals across the platform.

Is There a More Scientific Way to Calculate a Valuation?

We have discussed industry averages for valuations, but I haven't provided a model for calculating valuations. Why? Because the truth is, there are no precise valuations for early-stage companies.

The difficulty in valuing an early-stage business is due to numerous factors: the absence of comparable companies, the inexistence of historical data, the complexity of estimating volatility, and the large number of intangible assets, which unfortunately are key drivers for value in tech-related companies.

Just think about Facebook's first investor, Peter Thiel. He put $500,000 into the company when it had 1 million users and no revenue. If evaluated based on cash flow the company would have been worthless, but instead it was evaluated based on momentum, potential future value, and intangible assets—all hard numbers to quantify, and ultimately a very risky investment. But the risk Thiel took in making that investment ultimately netted him over $1 billion in cash upon the Facebook IPO.

Because of all of the unknowns involved in early-stage investing, professional VCs will often calculate a number of valuation models and scenarios and take a weighted average of them, as a starting point or an instrument for negotiations. That said, a deal will eventually happen at whatever price the market determines based on demand.

One way to do a quick check on what valuation investors might be willing to invest at is by determining what they think the possible exit value of a company is, based on the exits (liquidity events) of comparable companies. Using this exit value, the investors will determine what their ownership percentage would need to be at that point in order to make their target return on the dollar value of their principal investment (this is variable but may be between 10x and 30x). Taking into account any dilution that might happen in subsequent rounds, they then determine what the valuation would need to be now for their investment to give them that ownership stake in the company down the line.

In the end everyone tends to have their own rules. Angel investor Joanne Wilson said, "I like to own one percent of the company. And that one percent is at a $5 million cap and below. I really don't want to do investments that are over that amount."

Dave McClure says his biggest regret is missing the opportunity to invest in companies like Uber, LivingSocial, and Airbnb. For Uber in particular, he had the opportunity to invest at a $10 million valuation (the company is now worth over $50 billion). He passed on the deal because it simply felt too expensive at the time.

Investors on Risk and Valuations

"In startup investing, always think twice if something feels really cheap. Usually the best investments feel expensive."

—Sam Atman, president of Y Combinator [YC]

"I started making investments in companies that I felt were less risky but had also less upside. They weren't growth businesses but were looking for angel capital. I've actually found that the businesses that I thought were the least risky have been my worst investments."

—Elizabeth Krauss, angel investor

Types of Investment Vehicles

You have a few options when considering how you structure this exchange of capital for equity. Next we will dive into more details about each finding mechanism and how it facilitates the sale of ownership.

PRICED ROUNDS

Let's start by looking at priced rounds. A priced round is an equity-based investment round in which there is a defined pre-money valuation. In a priced round, equity investors will try to estimate the value of a company, then pay to buy a portion of the company's ownership at the valuation.

In priced rounds, investors receive their share of the company at the time of the investment. Our earlier example of a $1.5 million seed round at a $13.5 million pre-money valuation was an example of a priced round where the company would be giving away 10% at the time of the investment.

Priced rounds tend to involve a lot of paperwork, including the new investors agreeing on the terms of a shareholders' agreement, board rights, and a number of other terms we will get to later in the book.

CONVERTIBLE NOTES

Convertible notes are an alternative to priced rounds. They have grown significantly in popularity over the past few years, especially as a means of structuring a company's seed round.

Unlike priced rounds, where all terms are set at the time of the investment, convertible notes let you avoid going through a lengthy term sheet negotiation process and postpone setting a valuation on the company until later rounds.

Companies often raise convertible notes on a rolling basis, as opposed to investments in priced rounds, which are collected all at once. Most venture capitalists do not invest using convertible notes due to the uncertainty in the valuation.

But to angel investors and founders, convertible notes have their benefits. Convertible notes are usually relatively short documents with a limited number of conditions attached to them. They are structured as loans at the time the investment is made. The loan is automatically converted to equity when a later-stage equity investor appears, under terms that are governed by the terms of the original convertible note.

The three most important mechanics of a convertible note are the maturity date, the conversion valuation cap (or cap), and the conversion discount (or discount).

Maturity date

The maturity date is the date at which the loan will convert to equity. It does not affect the price of equity. Maturity dates are usually set well into the future, because investors would prefer to receive the equity rather than a repayment of the loan and because a maturity date set too soon may force a company to seek a funding round before it is ready. The conversion cap and the discount, however, can both have a significant impact on price upon conversion.

Cap

A cap is a way of giving investors who hold convertible notes access to equity at a reduced price. The founders of a startup will try to get the highest possible valuation for their company; however, the cap on a convertible note will set an upper limit on the valuation that is used to calculate the cost of equity for investors who hold convertible notes.

Let's imagine a company raises $100,000 at a $5 million cap. A year goes by and when the company completes its priced round, the valuation set by the new investors is $10 million pre-money. In this case, rather than the $100,000 resulting in a 1% stake in the business, as it would if the note converted at the full $10 million valuation, investors get 2% because the investment converts at the cap of $5 million (see Figure 3-1). The investors effectively get a 50% discount.

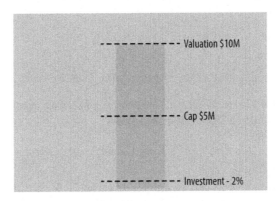

FIGURE 3-1. A $100,000 investment at a $5M cap on a $10M pre-money valuation gives convertible note holders a 2% stake in the company

If, however, the valuation at the time of the next priced round is lower than the cap, the investment is simply valued at the same valuation as it is to all new investors.

While an entrepreneur can try to raise on an uncapped note, most investors will be unwilling to invest. If a startup's valuation skyrockets and an investor didn't set a cap, the investor may find their note converts to equity at such a high valuation that they receive little to no equity in the company, despite the risk they took early on.

Discount

The discount, on the other hand, is exactly what it sounds like. It is a pre-negotiated discount on the price of equity during a funding round, generally around 20%. If the note holders in our previous example were to have a 20% discount, as opposed to a cap, they would receive their equity share based on an $8 million pre-money valuation rather than the full $10 million valuation set at the time of the priced round, resulting in a 1.25% share (see Figure 3-2).

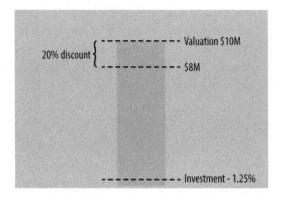

FIGURE 3-2. A $100,000 investment at a 20% discount on a $10M pre-money valuation gives convertible note holders a 1.25% stake in the company

When caps and discounts are combined, it can have a very significant impact on valuation.

Let's combine our two examples. Imagine a $100,000 investment, with a $5 million cap and 20% discount. If the company were to raise at any valuation above the $5 million cap, the investor would receive a 2.5% stake because the combined cap and discount decrease the valuation to $4 million (see Figure 3-3).

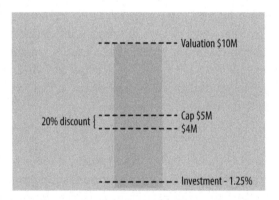

FIGURE 3-3. A $100,000 investment at a $5M cap and 20% discount on a $10M pre-money valuation gives convertible note holders a 2.5% stake in the company

In addition to the fact that convertible notes are faster and easier than priced rounds, involve less paperwork, and require no time spent setting a valuation, they have a few other benefits.

First, because you don't need to negotiate extensive terms when investing on a convertible note, you will save on legal fees, leaving the negotiation to the next priced round. Better yet, a lot of convertible note templates have been made available by well-known startup accelerators like 500 Startups and Y Combinator, which means you can even avoid legal fees entirely.

Accelerators

Accelerators are both investors and educators. Most accelerator programs write a small check to the companies they support and then put those companies through a regimented program. These programs are generally truncated into three- to four-month cycles (known as "cohorts" or "batches") from which the startups graduate. Upon graduation, startups participate in Demo Days, where they are given a couple of minutes to present their startup pitches in front of a curated group of investors.

Although the terms are often used interchangeably, an accelerator is different from an *incubator*. An incubator is formed when an external management team is brought in to manage an idea that was developed internally. Accelerators are much more common than incubators for early-stage companies. The best-known accelerators today are Y Combinator, TechStars, and 500 Startups.

The second benefit of convertible notes for investors is that the note is technically a debt until it converts. If the company goes bankrupt or fails to find future funders, then to the extent funds are available, the convertible notes will have to be paid back in cash—just like regular debt.

SAFES

As you can imagine, the fact that convertible notes may have to be repaid has made them much more popular among investors than among founders. To address this issue, Y Combinator introduced a new standardized legal document as an alternative to convertible notes, known as the Simple Agreement for Future Equity, or SAFE. Unlike a convertible note, a SAFE is not a debt instrument. There is no maturity date, no interest rate, and no threat of insolvency.

Founders can stack notes and SAFEs, issuing many notes on different terms. When issuing many notes, founders often slowly ratchet up the cap for each subsequent investor, or issue special terms to more coveted investors. While this may seem like an effective hack, it can cause quite a mess when it comes time to convert all the notes to equity. By stacking notes a founder can also run the risk of aggravating investors who were unaware that notes were being issued to their peers.

While many entrepreneurs lean toward convertible notes or SAFEs for early-stage funding rounds because of their speed and ease, the jury is still out within the investment community on which is better. Convertible notes and SAFEs leave a lot of ambiguity for both founders and investors. When a founder issues a convertible note, they don't know their company's market valuation, or how much of the company they have given away. And when an investor invests on a note, they are unaware of how many other notes have been issued, and at what price. Priced rounds are undoubtedly cleaner, because everyone involved knows what they own at the end of the day—and all aspects of the funding are negotiated.

 ## Template: Standardized Legal Documents

Looking for legal templates to start your fundraise? Visit *TheEntrepreneursGuide.com* to download standard legal templates put out by investors like 500 Startups and Y Combinator.

Conclusion

In this chapter we have introduced the mechanics of venture capital. We have discussed ownership, diving into cap tables and various classes of shares. And we have gone through the three most common mechanisms for selling shares. In the next chapter we'll take the knowledge you've gained so far and begin putting together a foundation for your funding round.

CHAPTER 4

Structuring Your Raise

Now it's time to take what you have learned so far about how financing works and start putting together a plan for your company.

In this chapter we will cover how you determine when is the best time to raise. We will go through what needs to get factored into the decision of how much to raise. And finally, we will determine the best legal structure for conducting your raise.

Timing Your Raise

Let's talk about the factors you need to consider in timing your fundraise.

The decision to raise may be precipitated by a number of factors. Perhaps recent company growth leads you to conclude that your company is particularly attractive. Perhaps there is a particular market opportunity that you want to capture that requires more resources. These are great reasons to raise because they are all positive signals about the growth trajectory of your company, and they will put you in a strong negotiating position.

While raising simply because you are out of money is certainly a legitimate reason, it is not the best reason, and it doesn't put you in a strong negotiating position with investors.

Let's dive deeper into the five factors affecting when to raise.

HAVE AT LEAST SIX MONTHS OF RUNWAY

Your company's *runway* is the number of months of cash you have left in the bank. As much as it's great to be idealistic about timing a funding round, there are some real limitations posed by your company's runway.

You need to raise money before you reach the end of your runway, or else you'll be out of money. When you're timing a fundraise, a common rule of thumb is to leave at least six months between when you plan to start fundraising and when you expect to reach the end of your runway.

The fundraising process can take six months, and the closer you are to the end of your runway when you hit the fundraising trail, the less negotiating power you will have, because investors will know you have no other options. If your company is profitable you have an indefinite runway, and running out of money doesn't have to factor into your fundraise, giving you more negotiating power.

If you don't have six months of runway left, you're in what Y Combinator founding partner Paul Graham calls "the Fatal Pitch." Your options are to decrease your costs or increase your revenue. If increasing your revenue is an option, do this first. If not, cutting back on costs, likely by letting go of employees, is your only option. If you find yourself in this situation, realize you are here—make changes to extend your runway, and then turn your attention back to fundraising.

UNDERSTAND YOUR SEASONALITY

Our second factor is seasonality. Businesses have seasonality, and how that will affect your metrics needs to play into your fundraising strategy.

Fitness apps do better in January, retail businesses tend to perform better in December, and dating apps do better around February. Don't be caught off-guard by seasonal changes in your business. While you are fundraising, investors will be tracking your business metrics. You want to use that seasonality to your advantage, rather than have it work against you. You want your numbers to grow during a fundraise, not suddenly plummet. If your numbers start going down during the fundraising, you might lose leverage in the negotiation, or begin losing investor interest. Know your seasonality, and plan accordingly.

PLAN AROUND INDUSTRY EVENTS

There are a number of industry events that can act as a way to either kick off a fundraise or create a sense of urgency for investors.

Great examples are the TechCrunch Disrupt Startup Battlefield, CES, the LAUNCH Festival, and the Web Summit Pitch Competition. Presenting at one of these competitions and performing well could give you the platform and media attention you need to start a raise. Securing a spot at one of these competitions could also help you get investors to commit prior to the event, by suggesting the opportunity might go away or cost more once you gain exposure there.

PLAN AROUND COMPANY MILESTONES

Companies should also be aware of events or milestones happening during their fundraise that might help to create a sense of urgency around their round.

Do you have a product launch coming up? Are you about to hit a particular traction milestone that will make you more appealing to investors? Do you have a major partnership you're about to close?

You can use these milestones as ways of either kicking off a fundraising process or getting investors to commit.

AVOID HOLIDAYS

Finally, holidays in the venture capital industry should factor into the timing of your raise. The venture capital world in most countries shuts down every July and August and from the US Thanksgiving holiday at the end of November until the new year. During this time, venture capitalists, and most angel investors, go on vacation and are slower to respond to email.

Starting a fundraise or trying to close a funding round during these times can be ill advised. Assuming you'll need at least two months from when you start pitching to when you close all of your commitments, the best months to start pitching are September, October, January, February, March, April, and May.

How Much to Raise

Once you know when you want to raise, you need to tackle how much you need to raise. The average seed round is between $360 and $1.5 million.

Many experts recommend that once you've decided to do a fundraise, you should raise as much money as possible so long as you are able to maintain control at any cost, and don't lose sight of what your liquidation preference would be in the case of an exit.

But remember that it's better from a perception standpoint to set a modest funding target and exceed it than to set an ambitious target and fail to hit it—not to mention the fact that the more money you raise, the more limited your exit opportunities will be. Also, more money generally means a higher bar if you ever raise money again.

Because of this, I'd recommend that rather than raising as much as possible, you raise enough money to get your company to the next inflection point (where you either have the metrics needed to raise a new round or are profitable). A common rule of thumb is that you should raise at least enough capital to last 18 months.

(TIP) The Startup Growth Calculator

The Startup Growth Calculator (*http://growth.tlb.org*) is a great online tool built by Trevor Blackwell, a founding partner at Y Combinator, to help startups determine how much money they need to raise to reach breakeven—or profitability. Once you reach breakeven, you have an infinite runway and can control your own funding destiny.

You do not want to be caught at the end of your funding without having hit the necessary milestones to either sustain yourself or attract new investment dollars. So, it is better to err on the side of caution when budgeting for a funding round.

Bridge Rounds

When a company fails to hit the milestones needed to raise its next round before running out of capital, it will often try to raise a bridge round. Bridge rounds are short-term loans that are used until a company secures permanent financing. This type of financing allows the user to meet current obligations by providing immediate cash flow. *Bridge rounds are to be avoided.* This is one of the reasons why estimating how much cash you need to reach your next funding milestone is so important.

Because entrepreneurs are usually at a negotiating disadvantage when raising bridge rounds, these rounds tend to come with very unfavorable terms, often forcing an entrepreneur to give up more equity and in some cases forcing a down round—which, as discussed earlier, can result in very punitive dilution for early shareholders.

Structuring a Funding Round

No matter when you decide to raise, and no matter what your target funding goal is, the third step in planning your raise is deciding how to structure the sale of the new shares. You'll most likely be deciding between the three most popular ways to structure a funding round that we discussed in Chapter 3:

Priced rounds
> An equity-based investment round in which there is a defined pre-money valuation

Convertible notes
> A debt-based financing where money is given as a loan at the time the investment is made, with the expectation that it will convert to equity at a later date

SAFEs (Simple Agreements for Future Equity)
> A simplified alternative to convertible notes

In a priced round, lead investors usually set the terms of the round. A lead investor may be an angel investor (probably one investing a fairly significant amount into the company) but more likely is an institutional investor. The lead investor will lay out these terms in a term sheet, which will be presented to the entrepreneur. On a million-dollar seed round a lead investor would usually put in at least $100,000, with half the round being ideal.

In a convertible note or SAFE round, the entrepreneur will have set an initial cap and discount that they wish to raise the round on. These numbers may be negotiated by the first investors who commit to the round, but it is a fairly simple negotiation.

Review Chapter 3 for guidance on standard valuation caps and discounts in today's market. Ultimately, every company is different, but the market averages and best practices that we've covered in these chapters are a great place to start.

Conclusion

In this chapter we have put together an initial structure for your fundraise. We have also concluded the first section of the book, building a foundational knowledge of venture capital. Let's review some of the core concepts covered so far.

Once you have decided when to raise, determined how much to raise, and settled on a structure for raising your round, you are ready to start preparing to pitch to investors. No matter which way you choose to structure your fundraise, the core principles of how you prepare to pitch, plan your raise, source investors, and execute your raise will remain quite similar. In the next part of the book, we will discuss how to prepare yourself to hit the fundraising trail.

Exercise: Planning Your Raise

In this exercise you'll answer the most important questions involved in structuring your fundraise.

- How much do you plan to raise?
    - $500K
    - $750K
    - $1M
    - $1.25M
    - $1.5M
    - Other _____

- When do you plan to start fundraising? (Remember to avoid holidays and leave three to six months to complete your raise.)

Jan	Feb	Mar	April	May	Jun
Jul	Aug	Sep	Oct	Nov	Dec

- What mechanism do you plan to use to raise?
    - Priced round
    - Convertible note
    - SAFE

Why is that mechanism right for you?

_____

_____

_____

_____

- What pre-money valuation (or cap in the case of a convertible note or SAFE) are you targeting for your round?

    — $1M

    — $2M

    — $3M

    — $4M

    — $5M

    — $6M

    — $7M

    — Other _____

- How much are you setting aside as an employee option pool?

    — 5%

    — 10%

    — 15%

    — 20%

    — Other _____

PART II

Preparing for the Fundraising Trail

CHAPTER 5

What Investors Are Looking For

THIS PART OF THE BOOK WILL PREPARE YOU TO HIT THE FUNDRAISING trail, building the toolkit you'll need to successfully pitch investors.

What's in that toolkit? You'll need a solid pitch, which is made up of your online brand, elevator pitch, and pitch deck. And you'll need to prepare all the financial and legal information an investor might ask for when evaluating you as an investment opportunity.

But before you can create your toolkit, we need to explore what investors look for in the early-stage investment opportunities they pursue.

Early in the life of your company you won't have a lot of data. There will not be a long track record that investors can review and analyze. Without data, early-stage investors have to make decisions based on "softer" attributes, such as your team, your market, or your product. When your company is further along, you'll be expected to have much more data that will enable investors to conduct a much deeper analysis of your metrics and traction.

Here are four main factors investors consider when evaluating early-stage investment opportunities:

Team

Are you the right team to tackle this problem? Are you the team that is going to win?

Market

How big is the market? How badly does it need a solution to the problem you are tackling?

Product

What have you built? How far along is it? How does it compare to similar products currently in the market?

Traction

How are you performing on your key growth metrics?

In addition to the four main factors affecting investor decision making, we will also discuss the following considerations that will weigh into an investor's decision-making process:

Social proof

External validation

Geography

Where your company is located

The state of your corporate records

Whether your financial and legal house is in order

In this chapter we will dive into detail on each of these factors. As you read on, you must realistically evaluate your company on each attribute. Knowing how investors judge investment opportunities will be your guiding light as you prepare to make your first pitches.

Team

Most investors cite the team—more specifically, the founding team members—as the most important factor in their investment decision. When evaluating a team, investors look at five main factors:

Domain expertise

Domain expertise refers to your knowledge of a particular area or topic—specifically, the area in which you are founding your company. When evaluating a team's domain expertise, investors look at how qualified a team is to be working on the problem they have chosen. Do they have experience in the industry? Do they have some unique insight that no one else has?

Employment or academic pedigree

By looking at the companies or academic institutions a company is associated with, investors are able to make quick assessments of the team's quality and experience level. That said, these criteria tend to lead to a lot of bias, as investors tend to value companies or schools they are familiar with over ones they are not. As an entrepreneur, you should be conscious of investor biases. Research your targeted investors and try to position yourself in the best way possible for each one.

Team dynamics

Team dynamics refers to how well a team functions. Investors may look at how long team members have known one another and whether or not they have worked together before as a way of determining whether they'll work well together in the future. They will also pay close attention to the relationship and interactions between team members in meetings. Is there any obvious tension or misalignment between you and your cofounders? Is everyone in agreement about roles? Are you talking over one another? Is there a team member who is missing from every meeting? Take an objective look at your team dynamics, solve any issues, and be cognizant of how your internal dynamics may be perceived by outsiders.

Diversity of skills

When evaluating your team, look at what skills the founders have. Do they have the expertise needed to actually execute on their solution? If they don't, what is their plan to get the needed expertise? Avoid marketing your founding team as having similar skill sets. Be very clear about who will have what roles in the company, so that investors know there won't be tension over who gets to be CEO or CTO, for example.

The most common red flag for investors around this factor is a company without a technical cofounder, particularly if you are building a product that requires technical skill. Very often investors meet a founder or founding team with a great idea, but no way of executing it. It is frequently much harder to find technical people to work on the problem than a nontechnical founder may believe. Without a technical cofounder, it can be hard to understand the intricacies of your product, making it hard to hire and lead a successful product team. Be sure your team has the technical competency to execute. If you aren't technical, bring someone technical from your team to your investor meeting to add to your credibility.

Past accomplishments

Has your team built a company or a product before? Have you ever raised venture capital before? Is there some other notable accomplishment in your past that might reflect on your ability to build this company? Past accomplishments can help signal that your company's founding team has what it takes to execute on your idea.

Many venture capitalists prefer to back founders who have already had one successful exit. Not only do they feel this proves a founder is able to take a company from idea through to a liquidity event, but it also likely means that the founder has had enough personal financial success that they won't take the first acquisition offer that they receive. First-time founders find it hard to justify the risk of turning down life-changing money, whereas founders who have already had a successful exit are more likely to hold out for a bigger success.

If you are a first-time entrepreneur, it is very important to stress your commitment to building a *big* company. Don't talk about being excited about early exit opportunities, or mention that you think you'll be moving on to the next company in a couple of years. Investors need to feel confident that you have the ambition to build something big enough to provide them with the returns they are looking for.

In addition to these five main factors, investors will also factor in how much they actually want to work with you. Are you someone they want to interact with for the lifetime of the investment? Can they learn from you? Are you coachable? Finally, they will look at your company culture: how you hire, how you work, what your office environment is like. Is this a culture that they want to be a part of? Is it a culture that will be sustainable?

Red Flags

Now that you know how your team will be evaluated, let's talk about red flags. These are nonstarters that usually cause investors to shy away from particular teams. We already talked about the lack of a technical cofounder being a red flag to many investors. There are three more that you should consider:

Founders who are not working on the product full-time
> These founders are seen as not showing complete commitment to the project's success.

Married couples
> While there are a number of great examples of successful married couples that have founded companies (the cofounders of Eventbrite, for example), many investors see the presence of married couples as adding too much emotional and personal complexity to the business partnership.

Companies that have only one founder
> Solo founders are often avoided because investors believe this is a signal that the founder has been unable to convince others of the merit of their idea. Many investors also feel that solo founders are much less likely to succeed in the long run. There is not yet any conclusive data to support this, but the high number of large companies with multiple cofounders has led the investment market away from solo founders.

It is human nature to pattern-match and look for signals that help make our decision-making processes easier. Investors are no exception. You need to expect that investors evaluating your deal are not going to go through every aspect of your company in detail. They are looking for easy ways to identify that a team is credible. Your job as a founder is to assemble the best team possible and then sell that team to investors.

When describing your team, use short phrases. List the recognizable companies, brands, and schools that each team member is associated with. Name any past startup successes or past work the team has done together to show credibility and ensure that all key areas of expertise needed to execute the ideas are covered.

Exercise: The Dream Team

Imagine that you are an investor who is evaluating a team that is setting out to create a drone delivery service. What would the profile of the ideal team to start this company look like?

The team might consist of three Stanford grads (academic pedigree), who met in college (team dynamics). One of them was on the team that launched Google Express (domain expertise and employment pedigree), one was an early team member at 3D Robotics (domain expertise and employment pedigree), and one is a lawyer with government/lobbyist experience (diversity of skills). They have also started two previous businesses, raised over $30 million, and sold to Google and Amazon (past accomplishments).

Now look at your company.

What would the dream team executing your idea look like? How much of that aligns with your current team? Write a description of your team to position your team members in the best way possible. Investors don't want to invest in just any team; they want to invest in the team that is positioned to win. It should look like you were born to solve this problem. If you don't think your team looks like the team to win, identify where the gap is and consider recruiting team members to bridge it—or be honest with yourself about the gap and optimize on a different characteristic of your company when raising money.

Market

Once investors are confident in you and your team, they will turn their attention to the market in which you wish to participate. When evaluating your market, investors will look at three things:

Market size

Can your market support a big business?

Product/market fit

Are you building the right product to serve this market?

Red flags

Are there attributes of your market that might make it less appealing?

MARKET SIZE

Investors will be looking at whether your market is large enough to support building a big company, or, as we put it in Chapter 1, a unicorn, centaur, or pony. For most investors the magic number for a billion-dollar company is $100 million in annual revenues, which assumes an average of a 10x multiple on revenue upon acquisition or IPO. A market needs to be big enough to support a new entrant getting to $100 million per year in revenue within five to seven years in order to be attractive to investors looking for unicorns. A very simple rule of thumb: if your market isn't over a billion dollars a year, it probably won't support a billion-dollar company.

But while investors like big markets, they don't want to see a company trying to address such a large market that it can't possibly serve any one part of the market well; that shows that you aren't focused. It is better for you to start by focusing on a smaller market where you can meet all of the needs of your consumers. In time you can expand to take on larger markets as your product becomes more sophisticated. You need to be able to paint a picture that includes both your plan of attack against a small portion of the market and your grander vision for the company.

PRODUCT/MARKET FIT

Your investors will be looking for signs that you either have or are on your way toward having product/market fit. As we discussed in Chapter 1, product/market fit is a term first introduced by Marc Andreessen, partner at Andreessen Horowitz (commonly referred to as A16Z), a Silicon Valley venture capital firm. He defined product/market fit as being in a good market with a product that can satisfy that market. Product/market fit, or the lack thereof, is not necessarily something that you can measure. It is often more of a feeling.

Andreessen believes that the market can be the most important factor in a company's success. His belief is that "in a great market—one with lots of real potential customers—the market pulls product out of the startup." In markets with very strong need, Andreessen believes the market will be fulfilled by the first viable product that comes along. The product doesn't need to be great, it just has to basically work; likewise, the team doesn't even need to be great, as long as it can produce that viable product.

For Andreessen, the only thing that matters for startups in those markets is getting to product/market fit.

Without product/market fit, customers aren't getting the value they want, the product isn't spreading, and the company isn't growing. But with it, customers are buying, the company is growing and hiring, and everybody is talking about the company, from investors to customers to the media.

When raising your first round, you may not have reached product/market fit, in which case you will want to show that there is a path to product/market fit. Show that your company is tackling a big enough problem, in a big enough market, that customers will (as Andreessen would say) pull the right product out of your team.

Make sure that the market has a burning need—a problem people desperately need solved, even if they don't know it yet. Without that need, reaching product/market fit can be near impossible.

RED FLAGS

There are a number of red flags that can act as deal breakers for investors when evaluating your market. These include:

Shrinking markets

> Investors do not want to enter shrinking markets (e.g., landline phones or wired Internet). I was pitched by a company creating a product to bring Internet access to cars that don't come with built-in communications. Sure, it's a great idea right now. But what happens in 5–10 years, when every car has Internet access out of the box? More than likely, that company's product becomes obsolete.

Legislative issues

> Investors are also wary of backing companies in markets with large legislative restrictions that would impede their ability to grow.

One of the best examples of a company with a very appealing market from a growth perspective is Uber. Uber is disrupting the global taxi market, and possibly the entire transportation industry. Taxi companies in the US alone see revenues of over $16 billion a year. The taxi market had not evolved much in the decades before Uber. It was a market ready for disruption, a market previously untouched by the Internet age.

The Uber market, however, is also an example of one that has a lot of regulation. You've likely seen the legal battles being waged in cities around the world to ban Uber cabs. Early investors evaluating Uber and its market would have had to weigh the risk of entering such a highly regulated industry as part of their decision.

Product

To quote Paul Graham, "To be a startup, a company has to be a product business, not a service business." This is not to say that your company must build a physical product, but rather that you need to build something that scales without requiring custom work for each additional customer. Products that only grow through additional time or effort do not scale. You want to sell coaching software, not sell coaching services by the hour. You want to sell 2 million copies of a book, not get paid by the word.

Having a great product for investment means both having the product developed and proving that people want it. When we talk about product, we're not just talking about the thing your company builds or delivers, whether it be software, a physical product, or a service. We are talking about product in a slightly broader sense that includes the quality of the product or service your company offers, the business model behind that product, and whether it matches a market need. We need this slightly broader definition because a great-quality product that doesn't serve a need, or costs more to deliver than a customer is willing to pay, is not a great product.

Only a few companies can raise money without proving out their business model or product/market fit. Companies in this category are usually those that have built a truly outstanding technology, something never before seen, something that stands to change how we interact with the world or that will disrupt how an entire industry operates. They will have built something that has intellectual property value, even if the company itself never sold a unit.

Most companies don't fit into that category, and when investors evaluate a company's product, they will first determine if anyone actually wants it and then they will evaluate its quality. Investors don't want to hear that your product is coming soon, or almost complete. In this day and age, especially when it comes to technology products, good teams should be able to create prototypes without requiring significant upfront funding. Even hardware companies, through the use of cheap prototyping tools and with the help of platforms like Kickstarter, can create initial products prior to raising any venture capital.

Investors are looking for a product that is usable or at least demoable. Your product should be detailed and well thought through. You need to demonstrate that you are capable of building and that you have solved a problem.

 ## Oculus

Oculus, a virtual reality headset company recently acquired by Facebook, is an example of a company that was very appealing from a product perspective. Even in its earliest demos, the Oculus Rift, the company's first product, was able to clearly demonstrate a quality of virtual reality that many believe had never before been achieved.

Traction

Traction means different things to different companies, but in general it can be defined as the progress of a startup company and the momentum the business gains as it grows.

What investors are looking for when evaluating a company's traction is growth. Paul Graham has been known to tell companies going through Y Combinator's three-month accelerator program that they should identify the most important metric for their company and focus on growing that metric 10% week over week throughout the program.

At the early stages you may not have a lot of historical data, and good early-stage investors understand that, but they will still want to see evidence of momentum. They want to see that you are experimenting, iterating quickly, and improving—even if over a very short period of time.

When presenting to investors you need to showcase the metrics that matter most to your business (revenue, customers, usage, etc.) and show steady growth of those metrics over time. As entrepreneur and investor Mark Suster says, investors invest in lines, not dots. You want to show investors not just where you are today, but where you have come from and where you are going—proving that you are on a strong growth trajectory.

Kik

Companies that raise money largely based on their traction are companies that have been so rapidly embraced by customers that their metrics are almost unbelievable.

Kik, a mobile chat app that has now raised over $120 million in venture capital, is a great example of a company that caught investor attention due to traction. The app gained its first million users 15 days after it launched in October 2010, and its second million users just a week later. By September 2013 the app was at 80 million users and adding 225,000 new ones each day (*http://bit.ly/2ccSDm3*).

Startup Metrics

The most important traction metrics will vary from company to company, depending on stage, industry, business model, and much more. That said, here we'll cover the most common startup metrics cited in the fundraising process.

Recurring Revenue

While many early-stage companies do not have significant revenue, once you have started accepting any amount of revenue for your product, your revenue will be used by investors as an indicator of whether customers value your service.

One-time revenue can be a good indicator that customers are willing to pay for a product. But as an investor, you're most interested in recurring revenue.

Recurring revenue is revenue that is highly likely to continue. It is predictable revenue, often in the form of subscription-based contracts. Recurring revenue de-risks your business sales, and builds long-term value—value that will be very appealing to acquiring companies down the line.

For companies with recurring revenue, another important number that investors will look at is *churn rate*—the percentage of subscribers to a service that discontinue their subscription in a given time period.

In order for your company to expand, your growth rate must exceed your churn rate.

Active Users

Active users are counted by measuring the number of unique users during a specific measurement period. For example, monthly active users are measured by the number of users engaging with a product in the previous 30 days.

"Active users" is a very different number than "users." When you give investors a number of users, you are probably giving them the number of people that have ever signed up for or bought your product. The number of users will never go down. The number of active users, however, can go down, so if your company shows steady growth in your number of active users, you are giving a very positive signal to investors.

A company with strong recurring revenue growth should also show strong active user growth. If it doesn't, it could signal that the company has a very strong sales team, but a product that lacks stickiness.

Month-on-Month Growth

Startups are synonymous with growth. It is hard to make an accurate assessment of your startup based on the metrics of recurring revenue or active users without knowing whether those metrics are growing, shrinking, or stagnant.

The percentage by which your most important metrics grow between months is your month-on-month (MoM) growth. This metric will tell investors the trajectory of your company.

Addtional Metrics

In addition to recurring revenue, active users, and month-on-month growth, there are a number of other key metrics, not directly tied to traction, that every founder should know how to address when entering a fundraise:

Customer acquisition cost

Your customer acquisition cost (CAC) is the full cost of acquiring users, and is stated on a per-user basis. Not all early-stage businesses can reliably state their CAC, but investors expect you to eventually have a refined sales pipeline that allows you to predict exactly how much it costs you to acquire customers through each customer acquisition channel. Even if you are not at this point yet, you should know how to address the subject when asked for your CAC by prospective investors.

Customer lifetime value

The lifetime value (LTV) of your customers is the revenue from each customer each month, minus variable costs associated with servicing that customer, multiplied by the expected lifetime of that customer. Lifetime value is important because if it exceeds your customer acquisition cost, then you have a profitable sales funnel.

Burn rate

Your company's burn rate is the rate at which cash is decreasing. Almost all companies that have raised venture funding will experience negative cash flow. (The negative cash flow is, after all, why the company set out to raise money in the first place.) You calculate your burn rate by taking your bank balance at the beginning of the month and subtracting your bank balance at the end of the month. The result is the amount of negative cash flow, or your burn rate, for that month.

Runway

Understanding your burn rate is important because it allows you to calculate your runway. Your runway is the number of months of cash you have left on hand at any given time. You calculate your runway by dividing the amount of cash on hand by your burn rate.

Time to breakeven

The ultimate goal of a company is to make a profit. Your investors will expect you to understand how long it will take you to reach breakeven—in other words, when your monthly negative cash flow will turn into positive cash flow, a profit. To estimate your time to breakeven, you will need to prepare financial projections, something that is often requested during the due diligence process.

Other Factors Relating to Fundability

While companies are generally evaluated on the four main factors of team, market, product, and traction, there are also a number of other factors that can have a large impact on your startup's ability to raise financing. These other factors include social proof, geography, and the state of your corporate records.

SOCIAL PROOF

Social proof is one of the more fascinating factors that influence startup financing, and it is often incredibly powerful, especially at the early stages of a business. Have you ever looked at a funding announcement and not understood how the company could have raised money based on its current team, market, product, or traction? These companies usually raised with the help of strong social proof.

Social proof is a psychological phenomenon that occurs in ambiguous social situations. In these situations, people assume that others must have more information about the given situation than they do. In an attempt to reflect the socially acceptable behavior for that situation, they copy the behavior of those around them.

Funding rounds are ambiguous social situations where investors are looking for clues as to whether or not they should invest. In a fundraising scenario, social proof causes investors to believe that others have some information about a deal that they don't. If others begin supporting a company, investors generally take that to mean that the company is worth investing in, and will be more inclined to support the company too.

Let's explore some examples of social proof.

Past investors

Getting into a highly credible accelerator, or having a big-name angel investor support your company early on, can act as strong social proof and can make raising your first significant round easier.

Accelerators are programs that are open to companies by application only, and that provide both investment and guidance. Companies graduating from Y Combinator, arguably the most sought-after startup incubator in the world, tend to receive significantly higher valuations and raise money faster than comparable companies coming out of lesser-known accelerators or no accelerator at all.

There has been wide discussion online around what drives higher valuations for Y Combinator companies, and it can usually be attributed to advantages these companies have on the following key factors: access to information, access to capital, branding and validation, and increased valuations on angel rounds (*http://bit.ly/2cGZC6k*). Similar advantages can be created through notable or strategic investors.

Media

The media can be a very powerful lever in attracting investment interest. A company that is constantly mentioned in the press and attracting public attention will be more top of mind to an investor than a company they met with once and have not heard of since. Media will not be enough to close your round, but it can help speed up your fundraise or attract additional attention.

Your network/introductions

Investment rounds tend to spread through social groups. An introduction made by one of your investors to other investors they have strong relationships with, or whom they have coinvested with in the past, is very strong social proof. On the other hand, an angel investor or venture capitalist who is not investing in your company introducing you to another investor is negative social proof.

GEOGRAPHY

The top 15 startup funding hotbeds accounted for 74% of all venture capital financing done in 2014 (*http://bit.ly/2cCmJkd*), with the San Francisco Bay Area, Beijing, New York, New England (Boston), and Southern California topping the list. On a national level, the United States, China, Europe, India, Israel, and Canada top the list.

Despite the rise of platforms like AngelList, the increase in globally focused accelerators, and the growing number of startup successes outside of typical startup hubs, there is still a large portion of venture capital that is reliant on in-person interaction. The world is getting smaller, but geography is still a very important factor when it comes to financing. Capital tends to cluster, and investors rarely travel to find investments. To maximize your startup's ability to raise financing, you should base your company in close proximity to a funding hub.

Beyond simple proximity, locating your startup in a funding hub can be important because it can greatly affect the exit options for your company. When acquiring companies, most organizations want the acquired company to relocate into or in close proximity to their corporate offices. If your business has grown in a location where many of the biggest possible acquirers do not have a presence, your company might be overlooked for a possible exit opportunity in favor of a company that can be more easily relocated.

You should be aware of any legal restrictions around venture capital in your area. In addition to the added hurdle an investor might encounter simply trying to understand any legal differences between their region and your region of incorporation, there may be nonstarters that will make even the most dedicated investor turn away.

For example, Brazil currently has a very complex tax system and high taxes (*http://bit.ly/2cTPbzO*), which makes it incredibly difficult for Brazilian companies to compete internationally and restricts the likelihood of these companies attracting global investment.

A past example of a legal deterrent to investment on a geographical basis is that in 2010, changes in Canadian legislation (*http://tcrn.ch/2culmQJ*) allowed foreign investors to avoid producing hundreds of pages of documentation when investing in a Canadian startup. Until 2010 the original legislation scared most US investors away from investing into Canadian companies.

THE STATE OF YOUR CORPORATE RECORDS

One aspect of raising money that doesn't get discussed nearly enough is the importance of keeping good corporate records. That means keeping your cap table, your intellectual property records, and your financials in check, and having them ready to be reviewed by potential investors during the funding process. You don't want to be scrambling to get your house in order at the finish line.

Keep a clean cap table

As we discussed in Part I, your company's cap table will show your prospective investors what percentage of the company your shares represent (as a portion of the total number of shares outstanding).

Investors learn a lot about a company by looking at its cap table and will be looking out for red flags, like higher valuations in past rounds (indicating that you are raising a down round), low percentage of ownership for founders (which could result in low motivation), and inactive founders (people no longer active in the company holding large equity stakes, acting as dead weight on the cap table).

To avoid issues relating to inactive people on your cap table, don't give 20% to your mom, dad, aunt, uncle, or friend. Not only does it add dead weight to your cap table, but it looks unprofessional. Also make sure that all members of your founding team are put on vesting plans. A typical vesting schedule is a four-year term with a one-year cliff. On this vesting schedule, no shares will vest until the end of the first year, at which point all of the first year's shares will vest. Then shares will vest proportionately on a monthly basis until the end of the fourth year, at which point all shares will be held. Vesting matters because a cofounder leaving your team early on with 30% of the company could spell the death of any future funding rounds, or, at a minimum, a very large headache as you try to clean up the dead weight on your cap table when they leave. Vesting ensures that founders can only walk away with the shares they have vested up until that point.

While giving away too little equity in exchange for capital may lead to a down round, giving away too much equity early on for a small amount of funding will also raise red flags. Investors evaluating your company are investing in *you* and will be very suspicious of large equity shares for early investors—particularly if they believe those investors unfairly got a better deal than them, or if they feel the imbalance of equity will demotivate you, the entrepreneur.

If any of these cap table issues arise, the best-case scenario for you is that the investor asks that you clean up issues with your cap table before they will invest. In the worst case they may walk away from the deal entirely, either seeing the mistake as a red flag or simply not seeing the deal as worth the added hassle for them.

In any event, it's a preventable way to slow down or kill a funding round. Keep a clean capital table and be smart about how you give out equity at each stage.

Avoid intellectual property assignment issues

Before investing, most VCs will conduct due diligence on your company. The due diligence period for an investment generally happens after investors have committed to investing, but before the final paperwork is sent and the money is transferred. In the due diligence process, investors will be evaluating the financial, legal, labor, tax, technology, environment, and commercial state of your company.

One of the things that investors will be looking at when exploring the legal state of your company is intellectual property (IP). They're looking to see whether your company actually owns and has the rights to the product you have created. There are two key aspects of IP that VCs will be looking at in due diligence: whether everyone who has ever worked on your project has signed an IP assignment agreement and, for software companies, whether you have used any software in your product that you don't have the commercial right to use. These can be broken down as follows:

IP issues relating to people

How many people work for your company? How many friends and contractors helped you get the idea off the ground? Has every single person that has worked on your product or contributed key insights/

ideas to the project signed over all of the IP rights to the company (essentially saying that they no longer own the work)? If your answer to this question is no—or you're not entirely sure—you're not alone. This is generally one of those things entrepreneurs say that they will clean up one day and never do.

When you are closing a funding round, investors will want to see these IP assignment agreements and you will have to sign off that they are accurate and all-encompassing to the best of your knowledge. While yes, you can go back to any employees or contractors after the fact and get them to sign over the IP assignment rights, there is always a risk that they will not sign—or, worse yet, they will come back at you claiming ownership of the product.

Think of Mark Zuckerberg and the Winklevoss brothers in *The Social Network*, a movie based on the story of Facebook. The Winklevoss brothers cofounded Harvard Connection (later renamed ConnectU) while attending Harvard with Facebook founder Zuckerberg. In 2004, the brothers sued Zuckerberg, claiming he stole their ConnectU idea to create his social network site. They ultimately received $65 million ($20 million in cash, $45 million in stock) for their suit. That deal is now valued at over $200 million with the growth of Facebook stock value (*http://bit.ly/2cueENY*).

While IP assignment issues can usually be overcome, either through signatures after the fact or through settlements, they can be incredibly stressful and significantly delay the closure of a funding round. Be proactive. Avoid this problem and get IP assignment agreements signed every time someone works with you.

IP issues relating to software

Most software-based businesses today do not write all of the code running in their products. They use open source tools, languages, software packages, and the like to build and run their products— often hundreds of outside pieces of code are running in a single application. It is perfectly acceptable to have outside code in your product, given that the code that you are using has a license associated with it that allows you to use it in your application while still maintaining the right to use your product for commercial purposes.

Every piece of external code that you use in your product will have an associated license. You, or your developers, need to check the license on each of these. One of the more common, startup-friendly software licenses is the MIT license. This license permits reuse within proprietary software, provided all copies of the licensed software include a copy of the MIT license terms and the copyright notice. Some of the more popular software packages using the MIT license are Ruby on Rails, Node.js, and jQuery.

If there is something in your product with a license that does not allow you to redistribute it for commercial purposes or under the licensing scheme you intend to use, you need to get it out of your application, or you will not pass the due diligence process. Worse yet, if the error is not caught in your due diligence process during the fundraise, but is caught in due diligence when you are trying to sell your company years down the line, your acquisition deal could fall through.

Keep financials up-to-date

Either before investors commit to investing or during the due diligence period, they will ask you to send over your most up-to-date financial statements. You would think this would not be a hard request to meet. But the number of founders who find this to be a near-impossible task, having done little or no formal bookkeeping in the early days of their companies, is quite astounding. If you're one of these, you'll be sent on a mad dash to collect all expenses, receipted revenue, bank statements, and more and, either on your own or with the help of a bookkeeper, attempt to create these records fast enough that it seems like you had them all along.

For most, bringing the books up-to-date will just be a minor panic, solved with a couple of days of hard work. For others, such a request will expose huge gaps in their story—perhaps they are spending more than they realized or their revenue isn't as high as they had been reporting—creating a lot of confusion and doubt when shared with the investors. But no matter which category you fall into, such a scenario will be unnecessarily stressful and is entirely preventable.

Keep clean financial records at all times—you never know when you'll need to provide them for either a financing round or a potential acquisition. Find a bookkeeper from day one and have them on contract. You will not regret it.

Conclusion

In this chapter we have reviewed some of the key factors investors evaluate when looking at venture deals. While you want to present well on all of the main factors, investors tend to focus on your most exceptional attribute. Remember, your investors will be expecting decidedly above average returns—often a return of $10 for every dollar invested.

Companies that can provide these kinds of returns are not your average good company—they are truly exceptional; they are outliers. When a prospective investor is evaluating your company, they will want to know what makes it truly special. What makes it an outlier?

- Is it your team?
- Your market opportunity?
- Your product?
- Have you gained unbelievable traction?

A startup that hopes to attract capital must lead any discussion with prospective investors by precisely and positively identifying what makes the company truly exceptional. You will still need to perform well on the other investment criteria, but it will be that exceptional characteristic that draws investors toward your company.

Throughout the rest of Part II, we will use what you learned in this chapter to develop your fundraising toolkit—the tools you'll take on the fundraising trail to pitch your startup to investors.

While preparing to start the pitch process, don't forget how much your fundability can be influenced by factors outside the typical team, market, product, and traction. And remember that you don't need to be the best at everything—simply be exceptional at something.

CHAPTER 6

Building the Pitch

Your pitch is the story you tell about your team, market, product, and traction. It is how you describe what you do, why it matters, and why investors should invest.

Your pitch will take a number of forms throughout the fundraising process. It includes how you present your brand online, via email, and in person.

You can't expect your product or your numbers to speak for themselves. You need to know how to tell your story. No matter how good your company is, if your pitch is bad, you will have trouble getting funding.

Is your pitch well thought out and well designed? Are you professional? Are you able to inspire others to join you on your mission? Entrepreneurs who are good at telling their story are showing that they're good at business and at sales, thereby increasing investor confidence in their companies.

In this chapter we will build your pitch. We will cover:

- How to clean up your brand before you start pitching

- How to build an elevator pitch for your startup

- How to build a pitch deck

Cleaning Up Your Online Brand

First, let's talk about why your personal brand and your company's online image matter in a fundraise. As we've noted, for early-stage companies, investors generally have very little information on which to base their decisions. For this reason, investors look to assess the caliber of your team and your company by taking in as many data points about you as possible.

The first things an investor will see when you contact them regarding a fundraise are your email address and signature, your elevator pitch, and your pitch deck.

The next thing they will likely do is visit your company website, your LinkedIn page, your AngelList profile, and your social media accounts. They may also Google you and/or your company, looking for videos or recent media.

All of these things come together to create their first impression of your personal and company brands. Not having a personal or corporate brand is better than having a bad brand, but it will not do you any favors in the fundraising process.

Honing all aspects of your personal and corporate brands will help you package yourself and the way you'd like your company to be perceived. A big part of fundraising is optics. Strong brands can help establish credibility and show off your attention to detail, your ability to build connections and community, and your professionalism.

Now let's look at six ways to clean up your online brands.

LINKEDIN

Fully complete your LinkedIn profile. Collect references, get your number of connections over 500 (the highest number of connections LinkedIn will list), write a strong bio, list your current company as your current role, and include past experience. Note that a LinkedIn page that doesn't show you, or key members of your team, working in the current company will be a red flag to investors.

URL AND EMAIL

There is nothing worse than a long, hard-to-pronounce URL, or one with a bad extension (like *.net* or *.ca* for a business trying to serve a global consumer market). It's an equally bad signal for a founder to use a personal email address rather than a corporate email address. (Even worse is using a Hotmail address.)

Try to get a *.com* for your company. Set up a company email address if you aren't already using one, and add a professional signature to your emails that includes your phone number and role in the company.

SOCIAL

Secure Twitter, Facebook, and Instagram accounts for your company. Be active on your various social accounts, both personally and professionally. Investors will understand if a technical member of the team is not active on social media. But if your head of marketing or CEO has incomplete social profiles or little to no activity—or if a launch company has dead feeds—it will be a red flag.

Using something like Hootsuite to schedule tweets or Facebook posts for your company will help you stay on top of this if it's not something that comes naturally to you.

MEDIA

If your company is launched, you should make sure that there is recent, credible media for interested investors. If your company isn't launched, recent media about yourself, your team, and your past accomplishments can also lend credibility. Investors want to back a rocket ship—something everyone is talking about.

WEBSITE

Make sure your company website is slick. If your company is launched, the quality of your site and its design will signal to investors the quality of your product. Design is incredibly important. Invest in design—from your logo to your website to the skinning of your social pages. Investors will be judging your design sense at every turn. A well-designed brand signals that you will likely design a strong product, whereas poor design or an inconsistent brand signals that you will likely have a poor product design as well.

Investors will be understanding of prelaunch companies that don't have live websites, but even in that case they should still have a super-slick "coming soon" page. (GoDaddy coming soon pages are very amateur.)

Beyond just your company website, consider your personal website as well. In this day and age, a personal website can be a good way to instantly up your personal brand. Squarespace is an easy, beautiful site builder that can get you up and running in no time. In a time crunch, About.me can also work. Ensure your personal website includes your role at the company.

PHOTOS

Finally, invest in a photo shoot of yourself and your team. It's amazing what a few professional photos can do for your online image. You can instantly go from looking like you don't have a very put-together online image to looking like you have your stuff figured out. Take the half-day needed to do it right, hire a photographer, and give yourself and your company profile pic upgrades!

Elevator Pitch

Now that you've cleaned up your online image, let's talk about your elevator pitch. An elevator pitch is a brief speech that outlines an idea for a product, service, or project. The name comes from the notion that the speech should be delivered in the short time period of an elevator ride, usually 20–60 seconds.

A written elevator pitch should be one paragraph, no longer than a few sentences. An elevator pitch answers the questions "what," "why," and "how." You will give this pitch hundreds, if not thousands, of times when talking to customers, partners, employees, and anyone else in the industry. Your elevator pitch will be delivered both verbally and over email.

As you prepare for the fundraising trail, you'll want to make sure your pitch is tailored to investors. Keep your elevator pitch jargon-free. Avoid words like *revolutionize, viral, next-generation, synergy,* and the like.

A great place to start when coming up with your elevator pitch is by creating an "X for Y" description of your company—for example, "Uber for nannies." Instantly, people will know what that company does. It's likely an app that lets you call a nanny to any location, on demand.

The Pitch Deck

Unlike an elevator pitch, which is usually given verbally or over email, a pitch deck is largely visual.

An investor pitch deck is a 10- to 20-slide deck that covers the most important details about a company. It is built to help an investor quickly get a bird's-eye view of your business. Pitch decks are built in Keynote, PowerPoint, or Google Slides.

Your deck will often be emailed around ahead of meetings, and will also be presented during investor meetings; the presentation of your pitch deck is generally what people refer to as "the pitch."

You may have two versions of your deck; the one that you email around may include a bit more explanatory text and exclude any information that you don't want forwarded along.

(TIP) Tracking Engagement with Your Deck

DocSend and PointDrive are apps that have been growing in popularity among entrepreneurs for sharing their pitch decks with investors. Both apps allow you to send your deck as a link, rather than as an attachment, and provide interesting data on how people are interacting with your deck (such as who views your document, and for how long). The apps even let you turn off access to a document after you've sent it.

Every deck will be a bit different, but most pitch decks will cover the same high-level topics. Storyboarding your slides prior to making them is a good way to ensure that you are covering all of the high-level points, while saving you time on revisions.

Here is my recommended outline for an 11-slide pitch deck, plus appendix:

1. Title slide

2. Problem

3. Solution

4. Demo

5. Team

6. Traction/distribution

7. Business model

8. Competition/risks

9. Road map/milestones

10. The ask

11. Contact info

12. Appendix

Let's look at what you should include on each slide:

Title slide

The title slide should include your company logo, and a one-liner about what you do, your vision, and what drives you as a business.

Problem

The problem slide tells a story, outlining the current pain point in the market that you are solving. Use data to support how big this problem is, and the size of the business opportunity it presents.

Solution

The solution slide introduces how you are solving the problem and addressing the market need, effectively introducing your product. Talk about what makes you unique and where your insight comes from.

Demo

In the demo slide you want to show, not tell. Either jump over to a live product demo, or include a short embedded video (one minute or less) of how the product works. An embedded video avoids the chances of a broken demo and lets you control the narrative.

Team

The team slide is where you introduce your team, but more importantly it's where you tell investors why you are the best possible team to solve this problem. List relevant experience. Remember to use short phrases and recognizable companies and educational institutions where possible. Reference notable advisors or investors, if they are well known.

Traction/distribution

This slide is where you show your metrics. Create awesome charts. Make the slide easy to scan. Even if your traction is early, investors want to back metrics-driven founders.

Business model

This slide answers important questions like "How do you make money?" or "How do you plan to make money?" If you don't have a plan, be ready to defend why not, and describe what other metrics matter for you right now. For most companies, ad revenue (unless you already have it) is not a good answer here.

Competition

Avoiding your competition does not help you in a pitch. Your investors will find out you have competitors. With your competition slide, prove that you know your competitors, their strengths and weaknesses, and your competitive advantage.

Road map/milestones

Here you'll answer questions like "What's next?" and "What is your vision for the future?" Good milestones are product launches, users, and revenue. This is what your investors will measure you against in board meetings after you complete the raise.

The ask

In the ask slide, you'll explain what you want from the investor. This is where you talk about your raise, how much you need, and what you will use it for (e.g., product development, sales). How does this raise fit into the milestones you just discussed?

Contact info

This slide should include your name and contact details.

Appendix

The appendix is where you will put all the additional slides you think you might want to use in a meeting. Don't send your appendix out over email. Anticipate questions investors might ask and create slides to answer them. The appendix will include slides on topics such as financials, risks, legal status, past investors/advisors, IP, and the most commonly requested metrics. Having these slides ready in advance will make you look very professional and prepared.

What to Do When Preparing Your Deck

In this section we'll go through the best practices for preparing a great slide deck.

USE DATA

Investors love metrics-obsessed founders. Pull the investor into your story. Share your progress to date. Use numbers when discussing your traction, business model, and go-to-market strategy. Investors want to see how you think about your business, and they want to wake up the next morning still thinking about it. A vague, high-level explanation isn't going to pull anyone into your story.

PAINT THE BIG PICTURE

A great founding team has a vision of what the world will look like 3, 5, 10 years from now. You may be talking about your company today, but your investors aren't investing in today, they are investing in the future. Make sure investors come away from your pitch knowing the big picture for your business and how where you are today plays into that grander vision.

ITERATE

Your first pitch deck will not be perfect. Treat the pitch like a product; iterate on it until it is great. Your pitch deck will evolve. Note how investors react to each slide. Internalize the feedback and questions you get in investor presentations and continuously improve your deck, and your presentation, down to every word you say.

PUT TIME INTO DESIGN

Beyond just content, the design of your deck is incredibly important. If you can't build a beautiful, user-friendly slide presentation, why should investors believe you can build a great product? Once you've drafted the content for each slide, hire a designer to create your deck.

Don't have a designer on staff? Get someone you trust on contract or use an outsourced slide design service like SlideGenius, eSlide, Bright-Carbon, Presentation Elevation, or OutsourcedPPT—all of which specialize in designing slide decks. A beautiful slide deck is worth the investment.

 ## Sample Pitch Decks

Looking for pitch deck inspiration? Not sure where to start? Check out real pitch decks used by startups to raise funding by visiting us at *TheEntrepreneursGuide.com*.

Checklist: The Pitch Deck Design Checklist

Put your pitch deck through this checklist to ensure you're following pitch deck design best practices.

- ☐ Use larger fonts to keep it readable; 18-point font or higher is recommended.
- ☐ Where words can be replaced by a great visual, insert a visual.
- ☐ Make sure all charts are labeled properly.
- ☐ Slides should have supporting data only, not a list of everything you plan to say.
- ☐ The deck needs to be easily scannable. Slides should be clearly labeled: Problem, Solution, Team, and so on.
- ☐ Save the deck as a PDF. This will ensure the deck appears the same to everyone.
- ☐ Give your deck a version-controlled title, specific to your company: [Company Name] [yyyymmdd] (e.g., "Oreilly 20160424").
- ☐ Confirm that you have the proper license to use the images in your presentation. (Most search engines make it easy to search for Creative Commons images, and sites like iStockPhoto can be used to pay for licensing of copyrighted images.)
- ☐ Use a standard master slide design; all titles, sizes, and fonts should be consistent.
- ☐ If you list a statistic more than once, make sure it is consistent.
- ☐ Use standard numerical abbreviations throughout, like $1K, $1M, $1B.
- ☐ Round large numbers to keep the document clean and scannable.
- ☐ Because your presentation is designed to be projected on a large screen, use high-resolution images and high-contrast colors.
- ☐ Make sure all statistics are properly sourced.

What Not to Do When Preparing Your Deck

Now that you've seen some of the dos for preparing your slide deck, we'll cover some of the don'ts.

DON'T LIST A VALUATION

It's important to note that while a deck may mention how much a company is raising, it should not mention the valuation. Particularly in a priced-round raise, as a negotiation tactic you don't want to give the first valuation number. Only start mentioning valuation early if the round is already partially raised and the terms are locked.

DON'T INCLUDE EVERYTHING

The goal of a pitch deck is to pique interest, get investors excited, and kick off a conversation. It's more important to cover the parts of the company and the opportunity that get you most excited than to touch on every topic. Even the most introverted founders come to life when talking about what excites them about their business. Remember what we said in the previous chapter: startups should be exceptional. Make sure the exceptional characteristic of your company is what stands out in your deck. And don't worry about throwing in fancy animations between slides (it's distracting and unnecessary).

DON'T BE UNREALISTIC

Investors have a pretty good bullshit meter after seeing hundreds, if not thousands, of pitches. Don't pitch unrealistic growth. Yes, you want to be ambitious, but you also need investors to buy in. Your vision and your projections need to be believable. You need to get everyone in the room nodding along, not leaning back skeptically.

Spinning Your Story: How Entrepreneurs Deceive Investors with Vanity Metrics and Spin Numbers with Charts

Because it can be hard to show meaningful growth in revenue and active users, especially if you don't have product/market fit, many companies use "vanity metrics" as part of their pitch. Vanity metrics are metrics that might look good at first glance but have no bearing on the actual viability of your business.

Common metrics that startups will show to give the illusion of growth and success are signups, visits, time on site, or number of social media followers. While these stats might have real bearing on some businesses, for most companies they are nothing but noise. Vanity metrics are often meant to distract investors from the underlying issues with the business's more important metrics. In the long run, focusing on vanity metrics will cause your team to target and optimize the wrong things. In the short term, these metrics will do nothing but decrease your credibility with seasoned investors.

Another hack used by entrepreneurs is to present data in a misleading way, to make it seem better than it actually is. There are a number of ways to do this:

Using cumulative graphs to suggest growth

A hack used by many founders to bump up their numbers and make their graphs go "up and to the right" is that showing cumulative metrics, rather than month by month or week by week. When you show growth using a cumulative graph, it will always look like a company is growing. Companies that can show growth month by month are the ones that are actually growing.

Overlaying data sets to imply causation

Is it causation or correlation? Or neither? When two data sets that look similar are overlaid, we tend to assume they are related even if they are not (see Figure 6-1). Want to make an investor assume that the more money you pour into Facebook ads, the more revenue you make, even if you've never made a sale from Facebook? Overlay the data!

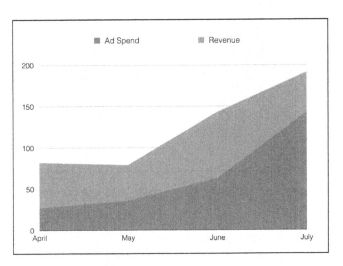

FIGURE 6-1. Overlaying two data sets that look similar can imply they're related even when they're not

Changing the perspective to distort data

There are many different ways to use the perspective of a graph to distort information (see Figure 6-2). 3D shapes are particularly notorious for presenting data in misleading ways. Want to make your very small market share look bigger? Change the perspective! Want to make the huge office expense you paid in 2014 look more reasonable? Create a cone-shaped graph!

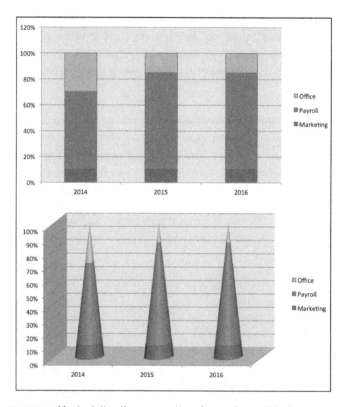

FIGURE 6-2. Manipulating the perspective of a graph can distort information

Changing the scale of a graph to exaggerate growth

The same information with a different x-axis can be perceived very differently. Only made a few hundred dollars more last month? Change the scale from thousands to hundreds (see Figure 6-3), and you'll look like you're growing!

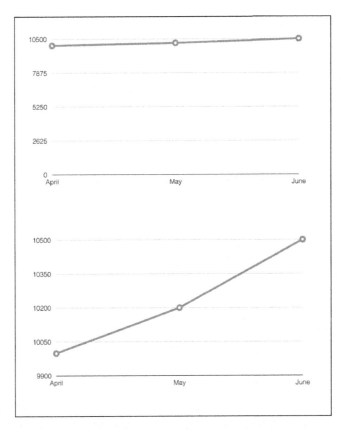

FIGURE 6-3. Changing the scale of a graph can suggest more growth than there actually is

While it may be tempting when putting together your pitch to use vanity metrics or deceptive charts, you should try to avoid using these tactics. Do you really want to raise money to scale a business that isn't working? If your answer is yes, it's important to understand the pressure you will be under to live up to the promises you made during the funding process.

Savvy investors won't fall for vanity metrics and deceiving graphs, but unsavvy investors often do. While "tricking" an investor into investing may seem like a win in the short term, remember that you'll be forced to work with this investor for the lifetime of your company. Not only are smart investors easier to manage, but naive investors that feel tricked may go out of their way to make your life difficult down the line.

What About Business Plans?

You might wonder why business plans haven't come up at all in the pitch prep process, so we'll take the time to address that here.

While writing a business plan can be a good exercise for a founder to understand their business, it is not something many venture capitalists will actually look at when reviewing a deal.

According to the *New York Times*, researchers at the University of Maryland's business school found that venture capitalists, who may be screening hundreds or thousands of companies each year, pay little or no heed to the content of business plans. Instead, the study said, because they make decisions "under conditions of high uncertainty," venture capitalists rely on instinct and their expertise.

Elevator pitches, executive summaries, and pitch decks are much more commonly reviewed. They allow an investor to quickly understand the key drivers of a business, without going through a 50-page business plan.

Conclusion

In this chapter we've covered everything you need to know to build your pitch—from honing your online brand to nailing your elevator pitch to building a pitch deck that will get investors excited.

In the next chapter we'll jump a bit deeper into the weeds, tackling two parts of the fundraising toolkit that often get forgotten or are left to be completed on the fly. We'll round out your toolkit with everything you need to make it through the due diligence process without breaking a sweat.

CHAPTER 7

Preparing for Due Diligence

You've nailed the pitch, and now it's time to focus on what investors will ask for once you've caught their initial interest. In this chapter we will complete your preparation to hit the fundraising trail.

Once an investor has expressed interest in investing in a company, the deal will enter into a due diligence process. "Due diligence" is a term given to the investigation or audit of a potential investment. Throughout the due diligence process, investors look to confirm all material facts in regard to a sale.

Almost all investors conduct at least minimal—and sometimes very extensive—due diligence on the deals they invest in. Investing in early-stage companies is risky, and conducting extensive due diligence can reveal problems with a company's business early on, allowing investors to identify the key risks associated with the investment. This will allow them to either develop a risk mitigation plan with the company or back out of the investment altogether.

Some investors conduct due diligence prior to issuing a *term sheet*, a nonbinding agreement used to propose the terms of an investment. However, most investors, especially when participating in more competitive deals, will issue a term sheet and then complete due diligence. For those deals, successful due diligence results in the legal paperwork being drafted and the investment round closing.

For investors, due diligence is a necessary evil. A recent study found that angel investments in which at least 20 hours of due diligence was done were five times more likely to have a positive return than investments made with less due diligence time (*http://bit.ly/2cHoxDL*).

How Due Diligence Is Conducted

The actual process of conducting due diligence generally takes the form of an extensive checklist. This list is sent to a startup by the prospective investor. As part of due diligence, investors also often request conversations with a company's customers, past investors, employees, and other key stakeholders. During due diligence, investors are both looking to confirm information presented in the company's initial pitch and to identify red flags. Is any information noticeably missing? Are there any inconsistencies? Does the company have legal rights to its product and trademarks? Is there anything disclosed during due diligence that might cause concern?

If there are red flags during the due diligence process, an investor can bring them up with the company. Many concerns can be easily addressed without materially affecting the deal. Other red flags may result in renegotiating aspects of the deal or, in extreme cases, canceling it altogether.

Responding to a Due Diligence Request

Your due diligence folder, also known as your "virtual data room," is a digital folder containing documents relating to your company and the requests made in the due diligence process. Sharing this folder is how you respond to a due diligence request. You will share your data room with investors when the due diligence period arises. Your data room will consist of an online repository of information in the form of documents, often organized into folders.

Dropbox is a great tool to use for your data room. To start your data room, simply create a *Data Room* folder on Dropbox and continue updating it with information as you prepare to hit the fundraising trail. Because Dropbox is always synced in real time, when you share your folder with investors the shared version will always remained synced with your version. Be sure to keep your data room organized. Clearly label folders and files. For extra credit with your prospective investors, customize your due diligence folder to match the checklist each investor has requested, naming each folder to match each point in the investor's list.

Template: The Funded Due Diligence Checklist Template

The most-prepared startups will prepare their due diligence folder before they even set out to fundraise, tweaking it slightly to match the specific requests of the investor.

Visit *TheEntrepreneursGuide.com* to download the Funded Due Diligence Checklist Template.

How to Prepare for Due Diligence

The due diligence process may sound a bit overwhelming, especially if you don't come from a legal or accounting background, but it is actually quite straightforward.

When a startup is prepared, with its due diligence folder ready, due diligence is much faster and smoother than if a company is gathering all of the information for the first time. As due diligence is fairly standardized, a startup can actually preempt 95% of the questions it will get during due diligence. Apart from just saving you a lot of time, doing this can have a number of other important advantages.

Preempting due diligence allows you to define the narrative rather than preparing information piecemeal. It will also make you appear much more professional to your prospective investors, solidifying their initial interest. Finally, going through the due diligence process ahead of a fundraise will force you to take a long, hard look at the inner workings of your business, exposing any weaknesses before you start pitching and allowing you to recalibrate before you start talking to investors.

How much information you are able to provide during the due diligence process can depend on the stage of your business. Earlier-stage businesses will naturally have fewer historical numbers and documents. The two primary types of due diligence that you will be taken through are *business due diligence* and *legal due diligence*. Both happen at the same time and are generally combined into one list in the requests from your prospective investors.

During business due diligence investors are looking to confirm details about a company's financial health, sales data, market, and team. Some of the things asked for in a business due diligence checklist are:

- Organizational charts
- Past financials and projections
- Management reports
- Stockholder communications
- Customer and supplier agreements
- Credit agreements and loan obligations
- Partnership or joint venture agreements

During legal due diligence, on the other hand, investors are looking into the structure of the company, its legal obligations, and its right over intellectual property. Some of the things asked for in a legal due diligence checklist are:

- A capitalization table
- Articles of incorporation
- Shareholder arrangements
- IP-related agreements
- Government authorizations

These standard documents should be easy for you to gather and place in your data room. However, there are other documents that you may be asked to provide that are more customized and may need to be prepared specifically for due diligence purposes. These include:

An overview of your customer acquisition channels
This would include an overview of your lead funnel and your customers by source, along with any information you have on your customer acquisition costs. If you have case studies of some of your key customers, this is a great place to include them. If you are a business reliant on larger deals, you may also want to be able to show a list of any customers in your current sales pipeline.

A spreadsheet with your key metrics
As discussed in Chapter 4, there are a number of key metrics that investors may request during the fundraising process. Prepare a spreadsheet with your company's core metrics for your data room. These key metrics may include your revenue, users, growth rates,

customer acquisition cost, lifetime value, burn rate, runway, and any other core metrics you are actively tracking.

A financial plan for the next three years

Projections are one of the key documents a startup founder prepares before hitting the fundraising trail. While your financial statements are a current snapshot of your business, your projections will tell investors about the expected future of your startup. These projections are one of the primary documents investors review during the due diligence process. Reviewing financials can help investors understand if a business has the potential to scale, while highlighting any gaps in the business.

Conclusion

In this chapter we have covered everything you need to prepare for the due diligence process. Being prepared will save you time and give you a better shot at success. Your data room—together with your pitch deck, your elevator pitch, and your new and improved online brand—will be your toolkit as you set out on the fundraising trail.

In our next chapter we'll dive a bit deeper into financial projections, a key part of your due diligence preparation that often overwhelms first-time founders and veterans alike.

CHAPTER 8

Drafting Financial Projections

CREATING FINANCIAL PROJECTIONS FOR STARTUPS IS HARD. OFTEN THERE is little historical data supporting the projections. Nevertheless, it is important to create projections in order to ensure that the founders themselves understand the inner workings of their business, and how it scales.

 ## Template: The Funded Financial Projections Template

Preparing financial projections can be intimidating. Luckily, we have a template to help! Visit *TheEntrepreneursGuide.com* to download the Funded Financial Projections Template.

How to Properly Prepare a Financial Statement

Financial projections are generally presented in the form of a spreadsheet. While the structure of the projections will vary greatly between startups, there are some common mistakes, exaggerations, and omissions that entrepreneurs tend to make in their projections.

Here we'll cover the ways to properly prepare your financial statements, and how you can avoid the common mistakes many entrepreneurs make.

LIST DEFERRED REVENUE SEPARATE FROM OTHER REVENUE

Deferred revenue is a liability that is created when monies are received by a company for goods and services not yet provided. Deferred revenue can help inflate a startup's numbers early on. It is important that financial projections be clear about whether there is deferred revenue included in financial projections. If it's not made clear, investors will likely ask.

LIST ONE-TIME REVENUE SEPARATE FROM OTHER REVENUE

Sometimes startups make money through hosting events, doing service work, getting sponsorships, and other one-time activities in order to keep the company afloat. These one-time revenue sources can be very misleading if they are not separated out from monthly recurring revenue.

Let's say a company makes $40K in August. You may assume they will make that in September too. But if $30K of that is from a one-time contract, their revenue may drop back down to $10K next month. Make sure financials clearly list where revenue is coming from.

LIST BOOKED REVENUE SEPARATE FROM OTHER REVENUE

Many companies will count revenue before it's actually in the bank. This could be service work that the company hasn't been paid for yet, or the pre-sale of a product that hasn't shipped yet. This type of revenue has some risk that it won't be collected and should be listed separately to revenue that has actually been received.

PAY CLOSE ATTENTION TO CASH FLOW

Make sure your financial projections include cash flow, not just the balance sheet or projections. In startups, cash is king.

BE CONSCIOUS OF OVERSPENDING

A lot of founders get caught up in the hype of what it means to run a startup. Beautiful offices, expensive perks, catered meals, team retreats; creating the Google experience.

While all of these things have their time and place, many companies introduce these perks when they simply can't afford them. This type of spending can drastically increase a company's burn rate, and should be avoided. Make sure the expenses listed in financials are reasonable for the geography and stage of the company.

PROPERLY HANDLE ASSUMPTIONS

A startup's financial projections include assumptions around growth rates, pricing, costs, and many other factors affecting the state of the company. The following tips will help you properly handle these assumptions.

Openly list assumptions

Financials that do not openly list assumptions are red flags to investors. The financials should include an extensive written explanation that describes the assumptions listed and how the entrepreneur arrived at those assumptions, including any evidence or supporting information.

Make bottom-up assumptions

You should understand the company's revenues and profits from the bottom up. The price of the product, the margin per unit, and the number of units sold should all match up to a revenue number.

How did you arrive at your assumptions? Were they pulled out of thin air? Or are they based on past growth or industry averages? Was the bill of material cost a guess? Or did it come from actual quotes? Numbers that come from credible sources will make for much more accurate projections and signal a more sophisticated entrepreneur.

Include scenario analysis

The only thing we know is true about a startup's projections is that they are wrong. It is a red flag if a startup doesn't include multiple possible scenarios in its calculations. Anyone reading the projections should be able to plug different numbers into the startup's assumptions, generally listed clearly at the top left of a spreadsheet, and see how different conditions might affect the company.

UNDERSTAND THE COST OF GOODS SOLD

Almost all companies have a cost associated with the sale of their product. The cost of goods sold (COGS) refers to the direct costs attributable to the production of the goods sold by a company. This amount includes the cost of the materials used in creating the product along with the direct labor costs used to produce it. Any costs associated with delivering a product or service should be included as costs in your projections.

ADDRESS BAD DEBT EXPENSES

Most businesses, including software businesses, will experience customers not paying for product that they have already received, leaving a bad debt. A great example is Uber. Have you ever taken Uber and been notified that your credit card payment failed to go through at the end of the trip? When this happens, Uber asks you to settle the debt before riding again. If you don't, Uber is out of pocket for your ride. Bad debts can have a material impact and should be addressed in financials.

SHOW LOAN PAYMENTS

Has the company taken on any loan obligations in its previous funding? If so, are these loan repayments shown in the financials?

INCLUDE TAXES AND BENEFITS

Many companies forget to include company taxes as a future expense (mostly because they are losing money and don't need to pay taxes now). But taxes can be a huge expense, particularly for a profitable company. Depending on where you are located and your corporate structure, you might expect to pay 25% or more in taxes. This can drastically affect projected profits. Many companies similarly forget to account for the fully loaded cost of employee salaries, once any benefit costs and employment insurance are factored in.

INCLUDE WIGGLE ROOM

Ensure some margin for error is factored in for both revenues and expenses. Again, the only thing you know about projections is that they are sure to be wrong, in one direction or the other. Be sure the company is prepared for that reality by either listing a margin for error in your expenses or slightly overestimating costs.

PROVIDE BREAKEVEN ANALYSIS

The ultimate goal of a company should be to turn a profit for its shareholders. Yes, startups that take on venture capital choose to run a loss to scale, but they should have a good understanding of when the company plans to reach a breakeven point.

This shows the entrepreneur has an understanding of the ultimate objective of the company. Reaching breakeven also means that even if the company chooses to raise another round of funding in the future, its fate will be in its own hands. In this case, failing to raise money will not kill the company, and it will be able to continue operating indefinitely.

INCLUDE THE FOUNDER'S SALARY

Founders often forget to include themselves in the company's expenses. While it's fairly common for founders to pay themselves little or nothing in the very early days of a company, this is generally not sustainable and not in the company's long-term interest. Investors don't want someone running the company if they are so desperate for money personally that they might accept the first acquisition offer—or worse yet, job offer—that comes their way.

Make sure reasonable compensation is included in projections. Geography and company stage tend to be large factors in how much a founder will be compensated. Compensation will be lower at the seed stage than during a VC round of financing and higher in more expensive regions like Silicon Valley.

There is no set rule for how much founders should be paid. But there are a couple of benchmarks.

According to Brad Feld, a VC at Foundry Group, typical founder compensation in its portfolio is $100,000–$250,000 in cash salary, with the CEO generally earning the most salary, plus a potential cash bonus of up to $100,000. That is in addition to founder equity (ranging from less than 1% to 20%).

Peter Thiel, on the other hand, believes that no CEO should be paid more than $150,000 per year. He says that his experience has shown that there is great predictive power in a venture-backed CEO's salary: the lower it is, the better the company tends to do.

INCLUDE BOTH HISTORICAL AND PROJECTED DATA
Many founders begin projections at month 1, leaving out all historical data. This can be very frustrating for investors who have no context for where your initial numbers are coming from. Rather than separating your historical financials from your projections, consider bridging the two statements by including them on the same spreadsheet. It will paint a much more compelling story for prospective investors.

OUTPUT KEY METRICS
While most entrepreneurs output financial statements from their projections, showing total revenue or cost analysis, few output any other key metrics that might be related to the financial projections, like acquisition costs or lifetime value. Outputting these numbers as part of your projections will show that you understand how all of your metrics tie in together, and will make it easier for investors to skim your projections for key insights.

Checklist: Financial Projection Formatting Checklist

Use this checklist when preparing financial projections to ensure your spreadsheet is readable and follows standard conventions.

☐ The document is designed for printing.

☐ All assumptions and key drivers are at the top left and can be adjusted.

☐ A legend of key abbreviations is included.

☐ Your spreadsheet is color-coded for easy scanning.

☐ Numbers are formatted consistently throughout (dollars should be formatted as dollars, numbers should have commas, and all cells should be rounded to two decimal places).

☐ A minimum font size of 10 points is used.

☐ The document is titled for version control: [Company Name][Projections] [yyyymmdd] (e.g., "OreillyProjections20150524").

☐ Tabs are properly labeled and organized.

☐ There is a separate section for key outputs (metrics, or statements derived from the statements).

Conclusion

In this chapter we've covered everything you need to know to create killer financial projections for your startup. Now that you have everything you need in your toolkit to hit the fundraising trail, in Part III of the book you will begin executing your fundraising. We'll start by planning the timing and structure of your raise. Then we'll build out a target list of investors and run a streamlined fundraising process, ending with money in the bank. This is where you make sure you're getting the most out of your fundraise.

PART III

Executing Your Fundraise

CHAPTER 9

The Investor Pipeline

MANY ENTREPRENEURS, PARTICULARLY FIRST-TIME ENTREPRENEURS, underestimate just how challenging the fundraising process can be. Maybe you think you can hire a banker to raise the round for you. Maybe you think you can put out a finder's fee and people will find investors for you. Or maybe you think you'll get a yes after a couple of meetings and don't think you need to set up anything else. But this way of thinking rarely works and usually does little more than waste time.

You are going to be the one raising money for your company. No one is going to raise it for you. Credible investors don't like dealing with intermediaries. They want to deal with and get to know the person who will be leading the company, and they don't like their investment going toward a finder's fee.

While a single investor can make up a round, rounds are usually made up of a number of investments from different individuals (angel investors) and institutions (venture capital firms), all of whom are buying into a company at the same point in time—generally on the same terms. To put together a round, the average entrepreneur literally needs to be in contact with dozens, if not hundreds, of investors before closing the round.

More than one major investor taking part in a funding round is known as *syndication*. Participating investors start out as a target list, and become part of your *investor sales pipeline* (or just pipeline), sometimes referred to as your *deal funnel*. A pipeline is a way of describing where your prospective investors are in the journey from initial contact through to commitment and then investment. Hundreds of investors might enter your pipeline, but only a handful will make it through every stage and end up as part of your round.

You can find many rounds today with more than 50 individual investors participating in a syndicate. While this may seem impressive, and while support from that many people may seem appealing, the truth is that selling and managing so many investors can be a logistical nightmare. Often startups are better off taking larger checks from fewer investors if they can.

In this chapter we cover the process of building a target list of investors and setting up initial meetings as part of your investor pipeline.

Special-Purpose Vehicles

An alternative to taking money from a syndicate would be encouraging your prospective investors to invest through a *special-purpose vehicle*, where many investors band together under one entity to invest in your company. The benefit of this option is that only one name actually ends up as a shareholder in your company, and fewer individual stakeholders need to be managed following the investment.

Types of Target Investors

Before we start building your target list of investors, let's talk some more about the two primary types of early-stage investors that you will encounter during your raise: venture capitalists (VCs) and angel investors.

Both venture capitalists and angel investors will be part of your target list of investors, entering the first stage of your investor pipeline. While both angel investors and VCs back high-risk, high-growth ventures, these two categories of investors have very different motivations for investing, and different vehicles through which they invest. Understanding these differences will help you better navigate the funding landscape as you build out your investor pipeline.

VENTURE CAPITALISTS

For many entrepreneurs, VC funding (investment from professional investors) is sought after. Getting investment from well-known or high-profile VCs can signal to the market that you have a high-growth company, at least in your investors' eyes.

A venture fund is any investment fund that invests in high-growth-potential, early-stage businesses. The amount that VCs invest can vary between each firm and each investment. This is generally dependent on the size of the investment fund and the stage of companies in which it invests. Some smaller VC funds invest as little as $15,000 in very early-stage companies, whereas later-stage VCs with much larger investment funds (sometimes over a billion dollars in investable capital) might invest tens or hundreds of millions of dollars in a single late-stage deal. When raising your first round, you'll likely be talking to smaller VC funds, sometimes referred to as *microfunds*.

Microfunds have grown significantly in popularity in recent years, and are now seen as a very important part of the early-stage funding landscape. Microfunds are small venture funds, usually with less than $50 million in deployable capital, which invest between $25,000 and $500,000 in each deal. Microfunds, or micro-VCs, are usually run by entrepreneurs or by former venture capitalists at larger firms looking to go out on their own.

Accelerators are a special type of microfund that generally invest even smaller amounts of capital (usually anywhere from $25,000 to $250,000), provide mentorship over a period of time, and take single-digit chunks of equity in very early-stage companies. Accelerators are a great way for new founders to get external validation and access to investor networks, considering the bar to getting accelerator funding is generally much lower than it is for getting other seed money.

ANGEL INVESTORS

Angel investors are not investing on behalf of a corporate entity or partnership. They are individuals, private investors, investing their own money. According to the US Angel Capital Association, the best available estimates are that about 300,000 people have made an angel investment in the last two years.

If your friends and family put money into your business, they are technically angel investors. While financial return is important to an angel's investment strategy, it is just one part of a wide range of personal motivations (which can include supporting entrepreneurs, learning about new industries, or making a change in the world). Therefore, their investment criteria and choices can be less predictable than those of VCs.

An angel group is one of the more common ways that angel investors are organized around the world. The US Angel Capital Association lists more than 250 angel groups in its member directory (*http://www.angelca pitalassociation.org/directory/*). Typically, angel groups are not funds; they are groups of individuals who share research and invest individually in the same deals. They also provide advice to their portfolio companies, much like a typical angel investor would. Even when part of a group, angels still maintain the ability to select which deals they wish to become a part of based on the deals vetted by the group.

The typical angel investor invests tens of thousands of dollars per investment. Extremely high net worth individuals can sometimes invest hundreds of thousands to millions in a single deal. Almost all angel investment is done only at the very early stage, when a company raises its first outside capital; in contrast, venture capital funds might invest in a second, third, or even later round of financing, depending on the firm.

Super Angels

Super angels are very active angel investors, often investing significantly larger sums of money than the typical angel investor. Most super angels are entrepreneurs themselves who have made their money through large liquidity events, such as an acquisition or an IPO. These individuals play an essential role in the innovation ecosystem.

An example of a super angel is Reid Hoffman, who in addition to having founded LinkedIn, has invested in many notable companies like Friendster, Zynga, and Flickr. A notable super angel couple is Scott and Cyan Banister, both entrepreneurs themselves, who together have invested in huge successes like PayPal, Facebook, Uber, Zappos, and SpaceX. On AngelList alone, their company has invested in 61 startups, seeing 25 exits.

As angel investments are made by individuals, the profiles of angel investors can vary dramatically. Not all types of angels are equally appealing to startups, as they vary in terms of their financial sophistication, risk profile, business acumen, experience, and the amount they can afford to invest.

For entrepreneurs seeking funding, the most appealing angel investors are former entrepreneurs and operators. These angels are seen to have the most relevant experience, and can add legitimacy to the companies they invest in. Other types of angel investors include industry executives and professionals in fields unrelated to the company raising money. The final class of angel for consideration is the entrepreneur's friends and family.

Legal Classifications of Angel Investors

Angel investors fall into two classes, accredited and unaccredited. Accredited investors, in the eyes of the law, are seen as being financially sophisticated enough to not require as much protection as unaccredited investors.

Up until October 2015, only accredited investors could be actively solicited for investment. However, new legislation under the Jumpstart Our Business Startups (JOBS) Act, which went into effect in early 2016, now allows companies to crowdfund up to $1 million from unaccredited investors, under some circumstances. Similar legislation is emerging around the world. It is recommended that you seek legal counsel before setting out on a fundraise to ensure your efforts to raise fall within regional security law.

In Canada, unaccredited equity investing is already in effect (with some restrictions) in a number of provinces. This is a huge step forward for the investment community. It is expected to have a dramatic impact on the funding landscape.

The requirements to be an accredited investor vary from country to country. In the United States, the SEC requires that accredited investors have: 1) a net worth exceeding $1 million, not including their primary residence; 2) personal income over $200,000 for at least two years in a row; or 3) joint income with their spouse of over $300,000 for at least two years. Similar standards exist for Canadian investors.

Creating a Target Investor List

Successful entrepreneurs will often need to meet with dozens of potential investors before filling their round. In order to get dozens of meetings, you'll likely need to start with 100+ investors on your target list, assuming some will not respond.

In order to manage the process of meeting with these investors, many entrepreneurs will build out a spreadsheet of prospective investors and manage the process much like any other sales process, getting introductions to leads and then following through to close the sale. ("Closing" in this case means getting the investment paperwork signed and the money in the bank.)

Template: The Funded Investor Funnel Template

SalesforceIQ and Google Spreadsheets are great tools to use when building your list. Looking for a template to get you started?

Download the Funded Investor Funnel Template at *TheEntrepreneursGuide.com*.

The first people to go on your list are investors that you are directly connected with through your personal or company network: family, friends, customers, mentors, or colleagues that might have the means and interest to invest. These close connections are most likely to turn into your lead investors, setting the terms for your round and starting the momentum needed to fill the round with other investors—likely investors you have less long-standing relationships with.

Once you've made a list of existing direct contacts, you will focus on investors that you want to target but aren't yet directly connected with. The best way to find new potential investors for your company is to mine online platforms like CrunchBase, LinkedIn, TheFunded.com, and AngelList.

Through these platforms, you have direct access to investors, and you can vet them based on activity, industry, and even the average size of their investments (often referred to as "check size") before meeting with them. That means more opportunities to meet with investors, and less wasted time in meetings with investors who don't actively write checks, or with investors who don't invest in your space.

Targeting Investors from AngelList

Let's walk through the process of finding target investors on AngelList:

1. From the AngelList home page, navigate to the People tab.

2. Go to the Role section and select "angel," narrowing the list down to investors.

3. Now you'll be able to see a list of investors that invest in your stage.

4. You can further narrow your search by filling out the Markets field, with whatever markets your company plays in.

5. You may also want to narrow your search by location, focusing on cities you plan to visit during your fundraise.

6. You could further narrow your search to investors you are directly connected with or that are in your network.

7. Go through this list and pick out names of people you've heard good things about, or who clearly get the space you are in, and then add them to your spreadsheet.

Evaluating Investor Fit

When putting together your list, you will want to make sure you are selecting investors that are a good fit for your round. When evaluating the fit of an individual at a VC firm or an angel investor, you'll want to look at a number of factors.

PERSONALITY FIT

The first factor you should consider when evaluating an investor's fit for your business's funding round is personality fit. Picking your investors, much like picking your cofounders, is like getting married. For better or for worse, you'll be working together until the company dies, one of you leaves the company, or you reach a liquidity event.

Your investors—especially investors with a position on your board— are effectively your bosses. You will need to listen to them and manage their interests. Bad personality fit will make you hate sending investor updates, avoid calls, and dread board meetings. Good personality fit will make running your company more fun, and make it much more likely that you'll have a productive long-term relationship.

DOMAIN EXPERTISE

Second, you'll want to look for investors that have domain expertise in your industry. You want investors that are knowledgeable about what your company does. They may have operated a company in the space, have invested in companies in the space before, or have related experience that makes them valuable to your particular business.

Someone who invests in consumer ecommerce may not be the best fit for a B2B developer platform. People who get what you do will be easier to pitch and more helpful as investors. They'll ask better questions and bring more relevant connections and advice to the table.

ACTIVITY

Unfortunately, many investors, angels and VCs alike, will claim to be actively investing—meeting with many entrepreneurs—but rarely actually write checks. These investors are wasting your time. Make sure the investors you're contacting have written a check in the last six months. This information is usually fairly accessible through AngelList and CrunchBase, but may need to be determined through direct conversations with the investors or people in their networks.

TRACK RECORD

Some investors have better financial performance than others. They have had more successes, are more respected, or are more connected in the industry. These are the investors you'd prefer to work with. You don't want to be working with investors that have bad track records or reputations, as it could affect your credibility. You can find out about an investor's track record by talking to entrepreneurs that they have funded or by reading about them online on sites like TheFunded.com and AngelList. If you are part of an accelerator, you will also find that alumni tend to be very open about sharing their experiences with investors.

STRATEGIC FIT

Strategic investors can add a lot of value beyond money. Is the investor well networked with one of your potential acquirers? Are they potential acquirers themselves? Can they open doors to new clients? Will they help to position you better in your industry? Some investors will give your business a strategic advantage, making them more relevant targets for your list.

STAGE

Stage relates to both your company's stage and the stage of the investment fund you are talking to, if you are talking to a fund.

When raising your round you want to talk to investors that are commonly part of seed and preseed deals and are comfortable being the first check into a company. You will waste time by talking to investors who invest only in later-stage rounds.

When it comes to fund stage, it is better to receive venture financing from a venture fund that is still early in its lifecycle. Most venture funds are set up to exist for 5–10 years. The first 3–5 years of the fund are the years during which the VCs actively invest, and the remaining years are the time when the VCs *harvest*, seeking a cash return from their investments to return to their investors (known as limited partnerships, or LPs).

The closer a fund is to 5–10 years of age, the more pressure you will face to provide a liquidity event. Not only will getting investment from a fund early in its lifecycle decrease the pressure on you to accept a premature liquidity event, but getting money out of a fund early (before investors have made all of their investments) also means that the fund will have more money in reserve when they invest in you. The more money the fund has uninvested, the easier it will be for you to go back to that investor and ask for follow-on funding.

TENURE

Tenure refers to how long an investor, typically a VC, has been with their current fund.

Some entrepreneurs might prefer to work with VCs who are respected but still early in their careers, people they can build long-term relationships with. Others may prioritize working with very seasoned VCs with more connections.

VCs who are just launching a fund, or starting at a new fund, can also be a great place to start because they'll be looking to make investments now to build their portfolios. That said, they may be looking for safer bets than would a VC with a long-established track record.

Different things will matter to different entrepreneurs, but it's important to be aware of tenure so that you can make an informed decision.

FUND HIERARCHY

The typical career path at a venture capital firm is very structured, and the primary roles include:

- Analyst
- Associate
- Principal
- Partner

Most established firms require that newcomers to the industry start at the bottom of the firm hierarchy, working their way up to partner. Smaller firms and younger firms, like 500 Startups, are usually willing to take a chance on newer players in the venture capital world.

Analysts are not part of the investment team at a firm, and are rarely involved in an investment decision. Associates are at the bottom of the hierarchy when it comes to the investment team. They usually do not have the discretion to write checks. When evaluating VCs and creating your target list, you want to be working with principal-level VCs and above, ideally connecting directly with partners who have the ability to sign off on deals.

Still, you need to be respectful of all people within a firm. Flat-out refusing to meet with an associate, or being arrogant or disrespectful to lower-level firm employees, will not go over well. Word about your behavior will travel quickly throughout the firm and the venture community.

Another very important role within the venture firm not listed here is the executive assistant. Executive assistants have a lot of power. They effectively control the VC's calendar. Be nice and get on their good side. They can get you a meeting, when otherwise the VC would have been booked—and they can make sure your email gets answered, even if the investor missed it initially.

EAST COAST VERSUS WEST COAST

"West Coast investors" primarily refers to investors in Silicon Valley. "East Coast investors" primarily refers to investors in New York and Boston.

West Coast investors are more laid back. They are known for 1) making more long-shot bets, 2) relying less on metrics, 3) basing their decisions more on potential, and 4) being more founder-friendly in their terms (higher valuations, cleaner term sheets). That said, West Coast VCs are less likely than East Coast VCs to participate in the earliest rounds of funding, preferring to invest after a prototype is created.

East Coast investors are known for 1) being more analytical, 2) relying more on metrics, and 3) having more investor-friendly, heavier term sheets. While there are always exceptions to these generalizations, understanding this difference may impact your impression of investor fit.

Making Initial Contact with Investors You Don't Know

Once you've developed a target list of investors, you need to contact them. Investors already in your network can be contacted directly, but you need to find creative ways to establish connections with investors who are not yet part of your network.

Let's talk about five ways to connect with new target investors.

JOIN AN ACCELERATOR

Accelerators give you access to a network of early-stage investors, and the best accelerators add a stamp of legitimacy to your startup. Joining an accelerator, particularly one of the top global accelerators, will immediately boost your prospective investor base.

Often, getting to your final investor intro may actually involve multiple layers of introductions and relationship building. In the case of an accelerator, that would mean getting introduced to someone who runs an accelerator, so that you can build a relationship and get into the program, and ultimately get warm introductions to its network of investors.

Even though accelerators look like they are open to all applications, the truth is that having an insider vouch for you can hugely impact your chances of getting accepted.

ENTER PITCH COMPETITIONS

The second way to connect with investors is through pitch competitions, where you have the opportunity to present your company to investors. Some of the more high-profile pitch competitions are Startup Battlefield, hosted by TechCrunch, and the LAUNCH competition, started by Jason Calacanis. You can often see which investors will be judging particular competitions ahead of time.

Just getting a spot on stage at one of these conferences, let alone winning, can be valuable in raising your company's profile. Like getting into an accelerator, getting a spot in a pitch competition may require that you have connections with the people running the competition.

GET WARM INTROS

The third way to connect with investors is through warm introductions, meaning you get introduced through an intermediary rather than by reaching out yourself. These days, most investors expect founders to use their networks to get introductions, which is why cold outreach is far down on the list of ways to meet investors. Whether you can get a warm introduction to an investor through your network is seen as a litmus test for your ability as a founder.

You can find out who in your network is connected to your target list of investors through LinkedIn, CrunchBase, and AngelList by looking at your connections. Another way to find out who people in your network are connected to is to simply show your target list to people you know and ask them who they could make intros to.

Don't request warm intros from investors that have turned you down. Unless there is a good reason (outside your company) for an investor to turn you down, them not investing will be a bad signal to the individual they are introducing you to. The best warm introductions come from your existing investors or entrepreneurs that an investor has already backed.

What you're aiming for in warm introductions is the *double opt-in intro*, meaning both you and the person you are getting connected with have agreed to the introduction before it is made. People don't like when intros are forced on them. The investor may take the meeting out of a sense of obligation, but not actually have any interest in the deal. This is a waste of time for both you and the investor.

To make a double opt-in intro, the introducer checks with you and the target investor to make sure you both want the introduction before making the connection. As the investor has effectively already said yes to the introduction, they are more likely to be responsive to you and the deal. It's a subtle difference, but an effective one.

Follow up on any intros immediately, adding further context and reiterating your ask.

The Forwardable Email

When requesting introductions, you want to make the job of the person introducing you as easy as possible. The best way to do this is through a forwardable email—an email from you to the person introducing you that includes basic information about you and your company that your introducer can simply forward along when requesting to make the connection, by adding a couple of lines of context. If the targeted investor agrees to the intro, your introducer can simply add you to the email.

Once you are added to the email conversation, politely move your introducer to Bcc, respecting their inbox. And for extra credit, continue nurturing your network by following up with your introducer to let them know what came of the introduction.

Sample: Forwardable Email

Subject: Intro to Roger Chabra at Rho Ventures for NewCo.

Jamie, thank you for passing this note to Roger.

Roger,

NewCo. is building a point-of-sale system for chain retailers. You can see a demo here, along with a case study of one of our pilot customers.

We are now being used by 20 retailers across the US and have a waitlist of 50 retails looking to implement the system. Our customers include chains like IndieFashion and RunwayStyle. Our customers have seen a large increase in efficiency and sales within their chain locations.

I've been following your blog for a number of years and appreciate your ongoing insights into the ecommerce space. I'll be in Montreal next week and would love the chance to meet and get your feedback on what we are doing.

Katherine

Investor and serial entrepreneur Dan Martell has an interesting spin on the forwardable email. He suggests forwarding an email not written *by* you, but one written *about* you by a very well-respected investor. By forwarding this email, not only are you making the job of the introducer easier by giving them the copy they need to request an intro, but you are also providing social proof that other respected people in the industry are making introductions for you.

ATTEND EVENTS

As we discussed earlier, timing your raise around big industry events can have its advantages, particularly when it comes to making new investor connections.

Most high-profile investors, both VCs and angels, attend many industry events and also speak at many of them. Look at what upcoming events your target investors will be attending, either by searching for them on event rosters or by following their blogs or social feeds.

Go to the same events, and make a point of introducing yourself. By meeting organically in person, you can establish a rapport and then follow up over email referencing the event, making them no longer cold contacts.

Events with smaller attendance, destination events, or events where there is a more casual atmosphere tend to be the best for creating lasting connections.

DO COLD OUTREACH

The final way that you can establish a connection with an investor is through a cold email. However, this method will have the lowest response rate of all the methods we've discussed.

Why are cold emails less successful? Investors receive a lot of emails. While most do their best to respond, often they can't respond to everything—so only emails that really pique their interest and seem like credible opportunities get a response, let alone result in a meeting. Your email needs to stand out above the rest.

How to Write a Cold Email

There are a lot of ways to write a bad cold email, so we'll touch on how you can structure a good one. In a cold email, you want to cover:

Who you are and how you found the investor
Make your introduction brief—one sentence—and then show that you have done your research on this investor, and that this is not a templated email.

Why you are writing
Are you asking a specific question? Do you want feedback? Were you encouraged to reach out by someone in the investor's network? Asking someone to invest in a first email is bound not to work, so give them another way to engage.

Your traction/vision/company, and why they should care
Make it clear what you do, explain why it's relevant to them, and get them excited.

Attachments and/or login details to a demo (optional)
> Provide a way for the prospective investor to get more information.

Next steps
> Are you expecting an email response? Meeting? Call? Be as specific as possible.

Increasing Response Rates and Building Rapport

When making initial contact with an investor, there are a few things you can do to increase the chances of getting a positive response. These tactics can be used to build rapport with both new and existing contacts. They will heighten your relevance to investors and boost your credibility.

FIND COMMON GROUND

First, you should look for opportunities to build common ground between you and the investor. Things, people, or interests you have in common with the investor will help you rise above the noise. Do your research, and understand what the investor is interested in both professionally and personally. Look for common organizations, cities, or activities that you can reference in person or over email to start building rapport.

ADD VALUE

Investors need things too. There are lots of ways that you can help an investor. Adding value makes you a legitimate part of the investor's network, and makes it more likely that they will reciprocate, perhaps by being more responsive, by providing advice/connections, or (ideally) by investing. Great ways to add value are to interview an investor for a relevant series or publication; regularly comment on the investor's blog with thoughtful, insightful comments; or engage with the investor on their social feed.

Additionally, maybe there are relevant introductions you can make for the investors or their portfolio companies that add real value.

MULTIPLE POINTS OF CONTACT

Another way to increase your relevance is to create more than a single touchpoint with an investor. Venture capital is a relationships game, and investors are unlikely to commit to an investment the first time they meet you.

You can create multiple touchpoints by arranging to attend the same events they will be attending, or by having your company in the news while you are raising. Each time you and your company cross the target investor's path will build your relationship with the investor, putting you higher on their radar and acting as social proof.

STAY IN TOUCH

The final tip for building rapport and increasing your relevance to investors is to stay in touch. After meeting with an investor for the first time, ideally before you actively start fundraising, ask if you can send them periodic updates.

If they say yes, send a quick note every time you hit a key milestone. Maybe forward along an internal update email, but be sure to personalize it with a short note to show you've taken the time to write to them personally. If you have a particularly strong connection with a potential investor, you may even consider asking them to join an advisory board. Not only will this keep you on the investor's radar, but this list of supporters can also become an incredibly useful resource to you as your company grows.

TIP Nondisclosure Agreements

A word to the wise on the topic of reaching out to investors: most investors, both VCs and angels, will tell you that they do not sign nondisclosure agreements (NDAs). Asking them to do so during the pitch process will simply make you seem like a novice.

Investors see hundreds of companies. Keeping track of what they've heard from whom and what is under NDA (and what isn't) would be incredibly difficult. Signing NDAs puts investors at risk. Furthermore, it is generally believed in the investment community that success is in the *execution* of an idea, not in the idea itself.

Founders who are overly protective of ideas are usually overestimating the significance of their ideas, or are creating very indefensible businesses that, once launched, could be replicated easily.

Timing Your Outreach

Once you've prepared your target list of investors, you're still not quite ready to dive into investor meetings. Rather than starting to discuss that they are raising immediately, many entrepreneurs start off with the *soft pitch*.

During the soft pitch phase, an entrepreneur tests the waters by taking meetings with investors for "advice"—using those meetings to gauge interest.

If interest is low, an entrepreneur may decide to hold off and go back when the company is further along. And because they never announced that they were raising, they avoid looking like they failed. If initial feedback is positive, you'll be ready to start publicly discussing a raise over email and in meetings. Begin to speak publicly about the fact that you are fundraising, and start the timer on your fundraise.

Mentor Whiplash

When meeting with advisors and investors for advice, you'll get many points of view. This can cause confusion, particularly for first-time founders. Who should you listen to? What do you do if you're getting conflicting advice? This is what people in the startup world call *mentor whiplash*.

The best advice for handling mentor whiplash is to be open to all of the feedback—collect all of the inputs—but don't immediately act on it. Think about all of the advice and information you receive, but ultimately listen to what your target market dictates above what you hear from investors and advisors.

If you can leave an early investor or advisor meeting having held your own, answering their questions to their satisfaction, leaving them excited about your business and the market opportunity, and gaining their support of your proposed funding milestones, then you are ready to proceed to the next phase of the fundraising process. If you aren't able to have confident discourse around the questions asked in your preliminary meetings and you leave the meetings feeling confused or questioning your direction, you aren't yet ready to go into pitch meetings.

The Initial Pitch Meeting

Once you send your first emails to investors on your target investor list stating that you're raising money, your timer is started. Your goal in your first email to an investor is to set up an initial meeting, or pitch.

These meetings will generally run 30–60 minutes. During a pitch meeting you will give an update on your company, discuss your raise, and gauge the investor's interest. The best pitch meetings are conversations, not presentations like those you would give at an accelerator demo day. Don't stand at the front of the room and give a choreographed talk. Use your slides as backup and have an open conversation with the investor.

You want to set up all of your meetings with potential investors within a short period of time. Meetings with potential should be set up in parallel, not in sequence. Taking all of your meetings at once creates buzz and urgency—investors talk to one another and will quickly see that you are in talks with many others. It gives the perception of momentum and prevents an early no from hurting you. Also, giving your pitch many times in a short period of time will help you hone it more quickly and give you confidence.

A common rule of thumb is that entrepreneurs should budget six months to conduct a fundraise. During those six months, fundraising can become an all-consuming activity for the company's CEO. It becomes very important that they have other members of their team who can support them during this time, either by assisting in the fundraising activities or by temporarily assuming some of the CEO's duties. Entrepreneurs at this stage in the fundraising process will be spending a lot of time in meetings with possible investors.

Checklists: The Pitch Meeting Checklists

These checklists will be your guide to a successful pitch meeting and follow-up.

Body Language Mistakes

Be mindful of sending out negative signals. Avoid the following body language mistakes:

- ☐ Weak handshake
- ☐ Avoiding eye contact or looking away
- ☐ Slouching

- ☐ Pointing your feet away
- ☐ Folding arms
- ☐ Not respecting personal space
- ☐ Fidgeting
- ☐ Appearing uninterested (or looking too intently)
- ☐ Forgetting to nod (or exaggerated nodding)
- ☐ Watching the clock
- ☐ Checking your phone
- ☐ Failing to mirror the other person's body language

Questions Investors May Ask You

You should be prepared to answer the following list of questions in investor conversations. Not every investor will ask every question, but practicing your answers will help you go confidently into your first meetings. Every time you get a new question from an investor, add it to this list:

- ☐ What problem are you solving and how are you solving it?
- ☐ What's your target customer?
- ☐ How big is the market opportunity?
- ☐ Who are your competitors and how are you different?
- ☐ What is proprietary about your solution?
- ☐ What are the biggest risks in your business?
- ☐ How do you make money now and in the future?
- ☐ How many paying customers do you have?
- ☐ What's a typical sales cycle?
- ☐ What other traction do you have so far?
- ☐ What is your current burn rate?
- ☐ How much did you spend to get to the current product?
- ☐ What are your next milestones for the company and the product?
- ☐ How much money do you need to hit those milestones?
- ☐ Could you grow faster with more money?

- ☐ Who are your investors so far? Are they also participating in the current round?
- ☐ How did you come up with the terms of the deal?
- ☐ How will you use the money you are raising to re-risk the business for future rounds?
- ☐ What is your customer acquisition strategy?
- ☐ Can I connect with customers who have used your product or service?
- ☐ Why are you the right person to start this business?
- ☐ Why is now the right time to start this business?
- ☐ Tell me something that's true, that almost nobody agrees with you on. (This is a famous question asked by investor Peter Thiel.)

Questions to Ask Investors

Here are some great questions you should ask your investors before they invest:

- ☐ How old is your fund?
- ☐ What is your typical decision-making process?
- ☐ How actively involved are you with your portfolio companies?
- ☐ How do you think you can help our company?
- ☐ How do you approach follow-on investments?
- ☐ How much follow-on investment do you think our company will need to succeed?
- ☐ What concerns do you have?
- ☐ What additional information would you like to see?
- ☐ What is your typical check size?
- ☐ Are there any other investors you typically coinvest alongside?
- ☐ What do you think of our founding team? What would you consider our strengths and weaknesses?
- ☐ Can you provide any references? (Only ask this after the initial meeting.)
- ☐ Can I talk to any of your portfolio companies that have failed? (Only ask this after the initial meeting.)

☐ How many deals have you personally brought in and closed over the past *x* years?

☐ How many boards do you currently sit on?

Post-Meeting To-Do List

After every investor meeting, use this checklist:

☐ Review feedback from the meeting.

☐ Follow up on any requests made by the investor in your meeting.

☐ Do whatever you can to make their next steps easier. Did they say they wanted to check your references? Have your references reach out to them. Did they have a lot of questions about your customer acquisition strategy? Prepare a quick slide deck walking them through the details.

☐ Update your pitch deck with any improvements that can be made before your next meeting.

☐ Update your investor pipeline with an updated status and any meeting notes.

Post-Meeting Mistakes to Avoid

Avoid these common mistakes when following up with investors after an initial meeting:

☐ Too many follow-up emails. Be concise and to the point.

☐ Asking for introductions to other investors after a pass.

☐ Going to another investor at the same firm after a pass.

☐ Falling off the radar.

☐ Not hearing no. Know when the investor is saying no, be gracious, and move on.

Things to Avoid When Pitching

This is your list of what to avoid in your initial pitch meeting:

☐ Broken product demos. Everything that can go wrong will. Make sure your demo is airtight; video is recommended.

☐ Rambling. Keep your answers short and avoid buzzwords.

☐ Trying to have all the answers. It's better to say you don't know.

☐ Not having a clear ask. Know what you want out of the meeting, and how much you're raising.

☐ Bringing nonfounders to your first meeting.

☐ Being disorganized. Be on time, have your presentation and demo ready to go, and bring a pen and paper.

☐ Trash talking (or not knowing about) your competitors.

☐ Not knowing key business metrics.

☐ Talking about exits. You are just getting started!

Conclusion

In this chapter we've gone through everything you need to know to build an initial investor pipeline and ace the first pitch meeting. It's important to remember that fundraising is like any other sales process, and a well-oiled sales pipeline will help you close the deal.

Many might even compare the process to dating. You have to kiss a lot of frogs, and you can't expect to close a deal after a single investor meeting. Start building investor relationships early, and nurture those relationships over time.

In the next chapter we will get into the details of what you'll ultimately be negotiating with these investors: the terms of your financing.

CHAPTER 10

The Anatomy of a Term Sheet

AT THIS POINT YOU HAVE BUILT AN INVESTOR PIPELINE AND ARE SETTING up your first pitch meetings. But before you can close the deal, we need to cover the term sheet.

When you are raising a round, the term sheet is the agreement that you hope to receive coming out of a meeting. It is a short, nonbinding document in which investors propose the investment and ownership conditions under which they would invest in a startup.

Generally (depending on your prior relationship), you will not receive a term sheet after your first interaction with an investor. It can take multiple meetings to build a rapport. That said, your ultimate goal when raising a round is to receive multiple term sheets, so that you can select and sign the most favorable one. Once you've reached an agreement and have a signed term sheet with a lead investor, you then fill the round with other investors.

Often when you are raising convertible notes or SAFEs, there is no term sheet phase. Term sheets are much more common in priced rounds. When raising a simple convertible note, you, the entrepreneur, can provide the first draft of the final agreement following your initial pitch meeting. The paperwork behind convertible notes or SAFEs is generally much simpler than that behind a priced round, requiring minimal negotiation around discount, cap, and interest rate and leaving most negotiation of other terms to the next round of financing.

Understanding the Term Sheet

You can prepare to review a term sheet by knowing what to expect and what you want out of an agreement. A term sheet can be an overwhelming document, but it is probably the most important document for you to understand—inside and out—when you finalize a deal.

Most negotiation in a deal occurs at the term sheet phase, rather than the drafting phase (the phase at which the final legal agreements are being written), and you can't always rely on your lawyer to get what you want out of a deal.

The term sheet does not constitute a promise to invest, but rather is a tool to facilitate a conversation between the investors and the founders about the conditions of a future agreement. The only portions of a term sheet that are binding are the *confidentiality clauses*, which commit potential investors to hold secret any financial or business information that the startup shares in the course of investment negotiations, and the *no-shop clause*, which prevents a startup from negotiating with other possible investors once they have signed the term sheet.

How Term Sheets Are Structured

A term sheet has three key sections: 1) an overview of the proposed deal and key players, 2) an outline of the rights and responsibilities of everyone who owns a piece of the startup, and 3) some housekeeping items that protect the value of the startup.

 ## Template: Term Sheet

Curious what a term sheet might look like when presented to you during a negotiation? A sample term sheet can be downloaded at *TheEntrepreneursGuide.com*.

THE DEAL AND KEY PLAYERS

The term sheet will identify the startup, its founders, and the potential investors. By the time a startup is seeking external investors, it should be a registered corporation and the term sheet will note where the company is registered—whether that's the US or another jurisdiction.

The term sheet will also note what kind of financial tools are being issued, whether that means convertible notes or shares, and at what valuation. Term sheets are accompanied by a capitalization table, which provides specific details on the total value of the company and who owns portions of it. In order for the company's legal team to create a cap table for a new transaction, the company must first share its existing capitalization table.

Finally, the term sheet will give a closing date, meaning the deadline by which a deal must be finalized, and the no-shop clause, which, as mentioned earlier, prevents the startup from seeking other investors while it is in negotiations.

It's advisable to place a limit on the length of the no-shop clause, in order to push the due diligence along faster. Four weeks is common.

RIGHTS AND RESPONSIBILITIES

Beyond those basic pieces of information, the term sheet will contain a number of clauses that lay out the rules of the road for everyone who owns a portion of the company—meaning the founders and investors.

This is the most important section of the term sheet and will ultimately turn into the *shareholders' agreement*, an independent and legally binding document.

Some of the terms in the shareholders' agreement will govern how big decisions about the startup are made. The most important of these relates to the *board of directors*, a body that votes on things like restructuring or selling the startup. The term sheet (and later the shareholders' agreement) will outline the composition of the board as well as the process for naming someone to or removing someone from the board.

A significant portion of the term sheet is dedicated to determining how ownership of the company will be managed through subsequent investment rounds, or outlining what happens if the company is closed or sold. There are many possible terms that could affect ownership. We'll talk about six of the most common ones here.

There is no right or wrong when it comes to a term sheet, but different terms will have different implications for you and your investors, some good and some bad. You need to understand these implications and optimize for an end result that is right for you.

Restrictions on transfer

Restrictions on transfer are rules about the conditions under which shareholders can sell or transfer their stake to another person. These exist to protect the startup and its investors by giving them a measure of control over company ownership.

Participation rights

Participation rights, which can also be called *follow-on* or *preemptive rights*, give investors the right of first refusal during a subsequent issue of shares. This means that the startup needs to give its existing investors first crack at buying into subsequent rounds. There is usually a maximum threshold that is tied to an investor's current stake. So, if an investor owns 15% of the company they'd get preemptive rights on getting to 15% ownership after the close of a future round.

Cosale rights

Cosale rights give investors a chance to cash out part of their investment. Cosale rights say that if the founders decide to sell a portion of their shares to a new investor, investors will have the right to sell an identical portion of ownership. This clause exists to align the interests of investors and founders, and to make sure that the founders can't cash out and leave investors behind.

Drag-along rights

Drag-along rights force investors to sell their shares in the event of a merger, acquisition, or other structural change to the startup. These terms exist to prevent minority shareholders from blocking or slowing down a transaction that would either let a successful company sell itself or give a failing company a way out.

Liquidation preference

Liquidation preference protects investors in a scenario where the company is being closed down and its assets liquidated. It gives them preference in the event of a sale.

An investor protected by this clause will have their initial investment repaid from the proceeds of the asset liquidation before any remaining cash is distributed among other shareholders. This kind of liquidation preference gives investors *seniority*—essentially it lays out how close to the front of the line a shareholder will be when the proceeds of a liquidation are handed out.

However, keep in mind that even if an investor gets liquidation preferences, they may not actually receive any money. Before any investors get repaid for the value of their equity, the company's debts need to be settled. There may also be other investors who come in later that take higher seniority, meaning they are closer to the front of the line and get cashed out first. There may be very little value left in the company and not enough cash to go around by the time it gets to shareholders with the lowest liquidation preference.

Founder vesting

Founder vesting, which we discussed in Chapter 5, is quite standard in venture deals. If you aren't already on a vesting plan before you set out to fundraise, you may be asked to go on to a vesting plan. Vesting requirements integrated as part of a term sheet are meant to address free-riding issues by incentivizing founder commitment to the company and ensuring investor and founder interests are aligned.

For founders who are not already on vesting agreements when they do a financing round, sometimes the vesting agreements will be backdated to when the founder started the company to give credit for time already served.

A clause associated with vesting that is more important to founders than investors is *acceleration upon change of control.* Having a vesting schedule that accelerates upon change of control means that in the event of the company reaching a liquidity event like an acquisition, the founder's shares will accelerate immediately.

For founders with vesting agreements, board composition and control (discussed in the rights and responsibilities section of the term sheet) become of great personal importance.

In addition to determining things like whether a company can accept a liquidity event, raise money, or give out stock options, a board can also determine salaries and when to hire or fire the company's management team. That means that founders who agree to a vesting agreement but give up board control open themselves up to the risk of getting fired and losing their entire equity stake if they are fired in the first year.

Founder board control means that the founders and their elected board representatives make up more than 50% of a board. A typical board composition in a seed round would be three board members—one elected by the founders (or common shareholders), one elected by the investors, and a final seat (usually someone independent from the company) elected by the founders, possibly with the requirement that the investors need to approve the election.

While this composition may be fairly standard, the number of board members and who elects them is entirely up for negotiation during the term sheet phase.

HOUSEKEEPING

Housekeeping items consist of terms that are often included in a term sheet that don't directly impact ownership.

These are standard clauses that exist to protect the value of the company by ensuring that it owns and safeguards its intellectual property. They also protect investors by ensuring that they receive timely information on the performance of the company.

Intellectual property rights

This requires the founders and employees to give the startup the rights to any intellectual property they created while working for it. Without this clause there is no legal restriction stopping an individual from taking key ideas or technologies to another company.

Information rights

An investor may receive information rights, which oblige the startup to share its financial performance and other relevant business information with them on a timely basis—usually quarterly.

Legal fees and confidentiality clause

It is fairly common that a company will agree to cover the investor's legal fees—with a cap on the amount an investor can claim being set out in the term sheet—and that there will be a confidentiality clause binding parties to secrecy.

Negotiating a Term Sheet

Which terms end up in the final term sheet is a matter of negotiation, and there are different formulations that are more favorable to the startup founders or to the investors. In order to get the best possible terms, you need to promote competition between investors. Your goal is to get multiple deals on the table, in a short period of time.

The process of getting the other offers must happen before you sign a term sheet and enter into a no-shop provision with the investor. It is during this phase that you are negotiating terms with investors to get the best possible deal. When negotiating a term sheet, be sure you have the counsel of an experienced startup lawyer—one who has seen recent deals and knows what is standard in your market.

Do not negotiate a term sheet point by point. Instead, you'll want to send over all of your recommended changes to a term sheet together. By giving all of your requests together, you can barter. There are going to be some items on a term sheet that will be very important to an investor but not matter much to you. When you give all your changes at once, you can strategically give in on list items that are less important to you, trading them for items that are more important to you.

Use the people in your network to gather backchannel information and use it to your advantage. Are you good friends with an analyst at a VC firm you are courting? Can they tell you what the investors said about you behind closed doors? Can the person who connected you with the investor get feedback on how the meeting went and pass that information along to you? These insights will help you follow up in the right ways and negotiate with more leverage on key terms.

Never tell a venture fund who else you are talking to until a term sheet is signed. VCs talk to one another. You want all the funds to be competing against one another to drive up your price and to secure better terms. Say no if people ask if you plan to build a syndicate of multiple VCs. You want other VCs to be their competitors on the deal, not their allies.

Exploding Term Sheets

Some term sheets get issued as *exploding term sheets*, meaning you need to review and sign them in a given period of time, often a few days. Exploding term sheets are designed to make it harder for you to get competing offers. You won't be able to control what type of term sheet you get, but you may look at investors providing exploding term sheets less positively than those providing nonexploding term sheets.

There are some institutional investors that don't put out exploding term sheets or use no-shop clauses. Fred Wilson of Union Square Ventures has said:

Don't pressure the entrepreneur to make a decision. Don't issue exploding term sheets. Don't put no-shops into your term sheets. Those kinds of things are signs of insecurity. I prefer to tell people that we'll have an exclusive relationship when the deal closes and not before then. If someone wants to leave me at the altar, better it happens then than after we are married.

Entrepreneur-friendly investors like Fred are loved by startups, but can be very rare.

Conclusion

Negotiation is not a zero-sum game. Your goal is to come out of a negotiation with a clean term sheet—one with simple, fair terms that are relatively standard in your given market. The terms should not be overly complicated or too heavily weighted in favor of the founder or the investor. Furthermore, there should be nothing in the document that will discourage future investors or impede the ongoing operation of the company.

While you want to make sure that you accept terms that protect your stake and your ability to earn a profit if the startup is successful, the best terms are ones that give everyone a stake in the future success of the company and establish a good working relationship.

CHAPTER 11

Closing the Deal

WE'VE DISCUSSED WHAT IT TAKES TO LINE UP INVESTOR MEETINGS, AND how to negotiate a term sheet—the document you hope to receive coming out of your conversations with prospective investors.

In this chapter we'll cover everything that happens between that initial pitch meeting and the deal being closed. The deal is closed when the paperwork is signed and the money is in the bank.

Securing a Lead

With investors that you have a strong relationship with, it may take just a single meeting to receive a term sheet or a commitment to invest through a convertible note or SAFE. But with most investors, a successful initial meeting generally leads to secondary conversations.

In most rounds, it takes one investor taking the lead and committing to the round before other investors start to come in to fill the round. Your number one priority in your early pitch meetings is to gauge who is most likely to lead, and get their commitment. In addition to being first in a round, the lead investor also generally makes the largest investment.

Rounds that include many investors, but no lead investor, are referred to as *party rounds*. Party rounds are not generally viewed positively, as they can signify that no particular investor believes in the deal enough to lead. They can also mean that when it comes time for the company to raise its next round, no investor is invested enough to help the company succeed. Party rounds are sometimes done out of necessity (you can't get one big investor), and other times they are done to have many high-profile names associated with a company.

Partner Meetings

When you're dealing with larger VC funds, what you're ultimately aiming for on the path to a term sheet is a full partner meeting. A partner meeting is a meeting where all partners at a venture firm are present, including the partner you have been meeting with (your champion). This meeting generally takes place on a Monday, because almost every venture capital firm hosts their partner meetings on Mondays.

The partner you meet with initially needs to become your champion internally for you to get a place at a partner meeting. In the best case, the full partner meeting would be your second meeting, but it can take longer to establish a rapport with your initial contact to get your foot in the door for a partner meeting.

Due Diligence and Drafting

If you're raising on a convertible note or SAFE, you may collect the investment documents and cash on a rolling basis as you get commitments from investors, or you may close them all at once. Minimal due diligence may be conducted by each investor, and no final paperwork beyond the note itself needs to be drafted or signed.

In a priced round, however, or any round involving a term sheet, once the term sheet is signed by both parties, you enter the due diligence process. At this point the no-shop clause will go into effect, and you will need to stop negotiating with other investors.

During this phase, due diligence is conducted by the lead investor. While term sheets are nonbinding, most respectable investors will not give a term sheet to an entrepreneur unless they are very serious about doing a deal.

Unless something material comes up in the due diligence preventing the VC from doing the deal, or making the VC want to renegotiate the deal, the deal should proceed. Likewise, entrepreneurs looking to maintain a good reputation in the investment community will not sign a term sheet unless they intend to go ahead and take the deal.

Filling the Round

Once due diligence is complete, the company and the lead investor will together begin gathering other investors to fill out any space left in the round. This is done through subsequent meetings and by going back to talk to investors that have previously expressed interest.

The amount of space left is the difference between the amount the lead investor is investing and your target fundraising goal. Other investors are usually much easier to get as your deal is already showing momentum and has the social proof of the lead investor behind it.

Sometimes when a company does not get commitments for the entire amount it was looking for, the round is left open even after the initial close. This allows the entrepreneur to continue to sign on more investors—similar to the rolling close of a note or SAFE round. The option of leaving a round open needs to be discussed with your investors and lawyers before the documents are drafted and the round is officially closed.

Drafting

Once all investors are committed and the round is full, the lawyers will begin drafting the documents to close the round. These documents generally include a share purchase agreement, and an investor rights agreement or shareholders' agreement.

Either the lead investor's lawyer or the startup's lawyer will do the first draft. The side that creates the draft has to put more time into the deal, but will have the advantage that they get to set the wording and structure of the initial contract. It's generally a good idea to offer to do the first draft.

The initial draft will be created based on the terms set out in the term sheet. This draft will then go back and forth between both sides until everyone is satisfied with the agreement. The company, as negotiated in the term sheet, will likely be covering legal costs for both its legal counsel and that of the investors.

During the drafting phase you want to control your legal costs. You can control your costs by avoiding overly complex terms, by using an experienced venture lawyer, and by taking the processes of drafting and reviewing the legal paperwork seriously.

Signing and Closing

Once drafted, the final legal agreements for the round will be sent out to all investors and the signing officers for the startup. These documents will include the shareholders' agreement, the details of which were negotiated at the term sheet phase. A deadline, usually a couple of days, is given to investors to sign.

Esignatures have become very popular in recent years, with services like Clerky, Signority, and DocuSign being the go-to esignature platforms. Allowing for esignatures can speed up your close, but make sure you check with a lawyer before proceeding.

Once the documents have been signed, investors generally wire their portion of the investment to the startup's bank account. It is at this point, when all docs are signed and all money has been transferred, that the round is officially closed. Final documents are sent out to all investors and share certificates are created.

Share certificates are physical pieces of paper listing the number of shares an investor owns. Institutional investors usually like to keep all of their own share certificates in their records. Angels and entrepreneurs may elect to keep their share certificates with the startup's lawyer.

Managing Investors

Once the deal is closed, your journey is just getting started—and your investors are now partners in growing your business. You are now running a venture-backed company, and it's time to start executing on your first orders of business.

Assemble your first board meetings, run strategy sessions, and begin executing on the plan set out in your fundraise. If you haven't already, share your hiring plan with your board and investors and begin bringing on new team members.

Stay engaged with your investors. Monthly updates are advisable, though quarterly may be acceptable; either way, be sure to make your investor group aware of the frequency with which they can expect updates.

Structuring an Investor Update

Good investor updates are easy for investors to scan for key details and make it easy for investors to help you when needed. Here is an outline of a strong advisor or investor update:

1. Highlights: What has gone well this month?

2. Challenges: What were the low points or challenges you faced?

3. Key Performance Indicators (KPIs): How are you performing on key metrics? Is this up or down from the last update?

4. Product milestones: Where are you in the product road map?

5. Sale and partnerships: Have you closed any notable deals? Are there any big business development deals on the horizon?

6. Hiring: Are there any new hires that have been made or are on the horizon?

7. Financing: What's your burn? What's your runway?

8. Press: List any notable press from the last month.

9. Asks: List specific things you need support on. Introductions? Help with a particular project? Additional funding?

10. Thanks: Give thanks to investors for their help with asks from the previous update.

Take advantage of your new support network and use the connections to build your business. Now is the time to request specific introductions and start networking with your investor's portfolio companies. Founders of your fellow portfolio companies can become customers, connectors, and part of your support network as you grow the company.

Startups should produce regular financial statements for their investors. Again, monthly is ideal and quarterly is acceptable, but anything less frequent can make it difficult to manage the company's cash flow and expenses on an ongoing basis. If the frequency with which you will share statements is not outlined in your investment agreements, establish this with your board shortly after closing.

When things go off track, don't hide from your investors. Be upfront. Your investors are there to help with real-time crisis management and would much prefer to know about problems early, rather than when they are much further down the line and time is running out.

Put as much care into managing your stakeholders now as you did while fundraising. Maintaining the support and connections of your first investors will be invaluable as you go on to raise future rounds of funding for your business.

Conclusion

It's important to remember that the fundraising process is the beginning of your relationship with your investors, and only one stage of your journey to building your company.

Take time to congratulate yourself, your investors, and your team on a job well done, but quickly turn your focus back to the company. If you're meeting your milestones, the next round likely won't be far off. If you're not meeting your milestones, that's all the more reason to keep your head down and focus on what matters most—growth.

PART IV

The Top Tens

CHAPTER 12

The Top 10 Tips for Equity Crowdfunding

EARLIER IN THE BOOK WE INTRODUCED THE CONCEPT OF *equity crowdfunding*, whereby contributors receive equity in a company rather than a reward in exchange for their money, and we mentioned some of the best-known equity crowdfunding platforms (including AngelList). Equity crowdfunding is a form of venture financing that takes place primarily online, and it has recently risen in popularity as a tool for early-stage entrepreneurs.

Both private investors and venture capitalists can invest through equity crowdfunding. In this chapter, we'll discuss how startups today are using equity crowdfunding platforms as a powerful tool for increasing the reach and success of their fundraising efforts.

Before we dive into our top 10 tips for equity crowdfunding, let's cover some of the equity crowdfunding basics. An equity crowdfunding platform is first and foremost a place where investors can discover investment opportunities and purchase an equity stake in those companies, by participating in a funding round. Because equity crowdfunding platforms cultivate a community of qualified investors, they are a great place to discover and close deals with investors outside your direct network.

There are numerous equity crowdfunding platforms to choose from, with the most popular options being AngelList, SeedInvest, and FundersClub. No matter what equity crowdfunding platform you select, the mechanics of running your crowdfunding campaign will be similar. Just as there is a formula for success on Kickstarter and Indiegogo, there are steps you can take to increase the likelihood of success raising on an equity crowdfunding platform.

Here are the top 10 tips for successful equity crowdfunding.

1. Prepare Yourself Legally

As we covered earlier, there are many rules and regulations about who can invest in startups, how they can invest, and how you can market to them. In general, most equity crowdfunding is still restricted to accredited investors. However, these regulations are changing quickly and you should always get legal counsel before diving into an equity fundraising campaign.

2. Pick the Right Platform for You

There is no definitive right or wrong answer when it comes to determining the best equity crowdfunding platform for your raise, but let's cover what you need to know to make an informed decision. The three primary criteria you should evaluate equity crowdfunding platforms against are curation, legal structure, and investor community.

Let's talk about the pros and cons of the three most popular online crowdfunding platforms (AngelList, SeedInvest, and FundersClub) as they relate to our assessment criteria:

Curation

Some equity crowdfunding platforms curate the deals that can fundraise on their platforms, while others let anyone participate. Being part of a curated group can add prestige to a fundraise, and curated platforms tend to have a vested interest in the success of the deals they choose to feature. AngelList is an open platform where anyone can post their fundraise. One way to differentiate yourself on Angel-List would be to get backed by a syndicate on the platform, as syndicates do curate their deals. SeedInvest and FundersClub, on the other hand, are curated platforms; you need to be selected by the platform in order to raise.

Legal structure

As we've discussed, there are many ways to structure startup financing. Equity crowdfunding platforms don't all structure investments in the same way. It's important to understand the legal structure and implications of a platform before diving in. SeedInvest and AngelList let investors invest directly into companies on the platform. FundersClub, on the other hand, joins individual investors together in a single-purpose vehicle built for investment in your company. As we've discussed previously, managing many shareholders on a cap table can be tedious, and the FundersClub model removes that complexity.

Investor community

The size and makeup of a platform's investor group is very important because it determines the possible reach of your campaign.

To date, AngelList, SeedInvest, and FundersClub are exclusive to accredited investors and US companies, but it is expected that many platforms will start allowing nonaccredited investors to take part in a portion of their deals in the coming year. Canadian-based Frontfundr is a platform that already accepts nonaccredited investors. Using a platform that is open to nonaccredited investors could lead to less sophisticated investors taking part in your round, but could also dramatically increase your possible investor pool.

AngelList has the largest community of investors and entrepreneurs, but SeedInvest and FundersClub (curated platforms with fewer deals) tend to put more marketing power behind the deals on their platform. If your company is not well known enough to stand out against all other startups in an open equity crowdfunding environment, then working with a curated platform might be to your advantage.

It's possible to make your deal available across multiple equity crowdfunding platforms. However, by doing this you risk cannibalizing your success on all platforms. It's generally better to put all of your efforts into one platform at a time. To the same end, avoid raising both online and offline at the same time.

3. Follow Other Deals

A great way to learn what works and what doesn't in an equity crowdfunding deal is to follow other companies. For at least a couple of months before you start raising, actively engage with other companies raising online through the various platforms. If you are an accredited investor yourself, you'll be able to see not only public updates, but also investor updates. Even if you can only see public updates, you'll still be able to get a sense of the tactics companies are using to market their deals, and the pace of their raises. Take note of how each platform varies, what works and what doesn't, and implement your learnings during your raise.

4. Work Directly with the Platform

Most equity crowdfunding platforms will work with entrepreneurs personally to help them craft their campaigns, particularly if they are excited about your product. Find out who the key employees managing the community at your selected platform are, and reach out directly to tell them about your campaign plans. Use metrics and past investors to get them excited. While some equity crowdfunding platforms, like AngelList, don't make you get approval before publishing a raise, it's still in your interest to get their support before listing, as it could lead to great advice and more exposure for your deal.

5. Create a Great Deal Room

Once you've selected a platform, you will develop sales copy describing your opportunity. You'll note how much you have raised to date and how much you intend to raise, and create a public version of your deck. This information will be entered into the platform to create your *deal room*— the place investors go to review your investment opportunity. Fully complete your deal room and ensure it is accurate and comprehensive. On AngelList in particular, many investors search for investment opportunities by industry or interest, so be sure to accurately describe your company and take full advantage of tagging functionality.

6. Time the Crowdfunding Portion of Your Raise Carefully

Your deal room will start as a private draft, and you will need to decide exactly when to make your investment public to the investor community. Timing when you make your deal room public is incredibly important. Equity crowdfunding is all about momentum. Don't publish a raise on equity crowdfunding starting from $0 raised; you need to show other investors that there is already interest. A good rule of thumb is to publish your deal on an equity crowdfunding round only after half the round is already raised, using the crowdfund to fill in the rest of the round rather than to kickstart it.

7. Get Backed by Influencers on the Platform

Equity crowdfunding platforms are social networks. You want to get backed (invested in) by the most influential users on the platform early on, in order to get maximum exposure for your deal. Target these influencers before you even publish the deal; have them soft-committed to the round before it goes live.

8. Take Advantage of Syndicates

On AngelList, not only can you get backed by individual investors, but you can also get backed by an online syndicate lead. When a syndicate lead backs you, your deal will be sent out to all of its followers. This can be very strong positive signaling and lead to a much faster raise than going out on your own.

Notable syndicates are run by the founders of AngelList, *Shark Tank*'s Barbara Corcoran, and 500 Startups.

9. Line Up Your Initial Backers

In addition to having momentum when you go into the online portion of your raise, you should have your first equity crowdfunding backers lined up before you go live. Take offline commitments for your equity crowdfunding raise, let these investors know when you plan to go live, and aggressively collect those commitments on the first day of your raise. An initial rush of investors when your deal goes live will create social proof for other investors considering the deal.

10. Be Data Focused

Equity crowdfunding platforms are a great place to showcase your traction. Because there are fewer personal points of contact, personal biases are often forced to take a back seat when investors are reviewing deals online—so your business can, more than ever, speak for itself. If you have traction, strong growth, and great deals in the pipeline, be sure to make that a major focus of your online pitch.

CHAPTER 13

The Top 10 Fundraising Mistakes

WE'VE SPENT A LOT OF TIME THROUGHOUT THIS BOOK MAKING SURE YOU know what to do when raising money, but now it's time to cover the top 10 fundraising mistakes that founders make when raising a round.

1. Waiting Too Long to Raise

When you set out to fundraise, leave yourself at least six months of runway. Avoid waiting for the next milestone, or the perfect time to raise, while running out of time and money. It could leave you without the necessary time to raise and result in premature death for your company.

2. Raising with Nothing More Than an Idea

There are very few people in the world who can raise money with nothing more than an idea. Generally, the only people who can do this are entrepreneurs with very strong past relationships, and a track record for building incredible products and making money for investors. Prototypes are easier to make than ever. Make sure you have at least a basic working prototype (also know as a *minimum viable product*, or MVP) when you start raising.

3. Putting All Your Eggs in One Basket

Many entrepreneurs raise in sequence rather than in parallel, putting all of their hope in a single investor issuing the right term sheet at any given time. You can't bank on a single investor to give you the best terms. Without a competitive environment, they have no incentive to give you better terms or commit. Take your meetings in parallel and create a competitive environment.

4. Overemphasizing the Importance of Valuation and Overoptimizing Terms

Ensure the terms you are getting are fair and in line with the market, but don't overoptimize. Get good investors. Keep the terms clean and get back to work. Yes, if you have leverage you can ask for what you want, but don't jerk your investors around or be disrespectful to anyone you meet in the industry. And don't ask for such a high valuation that you set yourself up for a down round in the future.

5. Not Hearing No

Many investors will never actually tell you no, at least so explicitly. They may be trying to avoid a socially awkward situation, or they may be trying to leave their options open to invest in the future. You need to read between the lines. Responses such as "Come back when you've hit x milestone" or "Let's talk when you have a lead" are ways that investors are actually saying no. In Sam Altman's words, anything that's not a term sheet is a no. Hear it, and move on.

6. Not Doing Your Research

Make sure you know who you are talking to when you email or meet with an investor. Make sure you know what standard terms are for your stage and industry. Not knowing the area of expertise of your target investor, what related companies they've invested in, what their experiences have been, and so on will make you seem very unprepared and unfocused in your fundraise. Asking for terms that are nonstandard, or valuations that are either way higher or way lower than expected, can also signal a lack of preparedness.

7. Not Having a Lead Investor

Not securing a lead will make the rest of your fundraise more difficult. Even if you are able to put together a party round (a round without a lead), it's probably not in your best interest. Having an investor truly invested in your success can be to your advantage, particularly as you plan for your next funding round.

8. Pitching Poorly

Your company doesn't speak for itself. You need to bring the story to life. A bad presentation, or a founder who can't express their excitement for their product, won't be able to elicit excitement from investors. Founder passion is contagious.

9. Prioritizing Money over the Right Investor

Not all money is good money. In fact, some venture money can be very harmful, when you get it on the wrong terms, or with the wrong investors behind it. Check the references of your major investors. In particular, talk to entrepreneurs they've invested in. Don't take money from bad investors. You'll come to regret it down the line.

10. Not Understanding Your Own Business

Not only do you have to be able to paint the big picture, but you also need to understand your key metrics, your margins, and your operations plan. Ensure you understand your own business before stepping in front of an investor. And if you miss something, learn as you go.

Bonus: Raising Too Much or Too Little Money

Raise enough money to get you to your next major fundraising milestone, and leave wiggle room for unexpected expenses or slower sales cycles. Don't raise so much money that you lose control of the company's spending or have a valuation so high you risk a down round in the future.

CHAPTER 14

The Top 10 Fundraising Hacks

FUNDRAISING IS A SALES PROCESS, AND LIKE ANY OTHER SALES PROCESS, much more than the fundamentals of a business opportunity can play into investors' decision making.

Fundraising is a bit of a zero-sum game. Investors have a limited amount of capital to give out; every dollar another company gets is a dollar that doesn't go to you. While investors can choose to invest in multiple deals at a given time, you are effectively competing against the other entrepreneurs raising money—for attention, time, and ultimately capital.

While the fundraising process itself is quite straightforward—get introductions, pitch, try to get multiple offers, and then close—many founders implement hacks along the way to get investors to commit faster, to encourage competition, and to get better terms.

Knowing what hacks other entrepreneurs have used, and what effects, both positive and negative, they can have on a fundraise, will help you make an informed decision about whether to implement any of these tactics in your situation.

Here are the top 10 fundraising hacks—why they work, and when they backfire.

1. Set a Deadline to Create Urgency

A common fundraising hack is to set a close date—either an arbitrary date or a company milestone—for your fundraise and state it publicly. Creating this deadline will force investors to act, making them commit faster than they might have otherwise.

The danger in setting a public close date is that if you aren't able to get your commitments by your cutoff date, you go away looking like you failed. You lose leverage in any future conversations, and you'll likely need to wait until your company's next milestone to hit the fundraising trail again (assuming you have enough money to make it there). Use deadlines cautiously.

2. Network Your Way to Investors Through Entrepreneurs

This hack is a fundraising tactic from Dan Martell. Dan's approach to getting warm introductions is to find companies on CrunchBase or AngelList that have raised money from the investors he's interested in raising from, and cold-email the founders asking to schedule a call with them for advice.

He develops a rapport with them, and then asks who their investors are and if they'd be willing to make an intro. This strategy could backfire, however, if a founder you reach out to doesn't like you or your tactics, and ends up sharing a negative opinion with their investor. If you choose to use this tactic, put as much effort into building a rapport with the founders as you would with an investor. Do your best to make the relationship reciprocal. Don't just ask for things for yourself; have something to offer them too—like introductions that might be useful to them in growing their business.

3. Time Media Around a Raise

Timing big media announcements to happen around your fundraise can help drive investor interest and provide social proof to investors. Publications that investors read (such as TechCrunch) are the best places to target for such announcements.

There isn't really a downside to timing media around your fundraise, apart from the fact that coordinating media, and possibly the launch of features associated with that media, could distract you from executing your fundraise.

4. Inflate Demand

Make yourself seem more in demand than you actually are. For example, claim your schedule is really packed except for one specific hour, or claim you are only in town for a limited time. Investors want what they can't have.

Inflating demand usually works to pique investor interest, but if you aren't able to raise, it may make you look worse (as it appeared that you were in many pitch meetings).

5. Play Investors Against One Another

An example of playing investors off one another would be casually mentioning to one investor that you'll be having dinner with another investor. People are inherently competitive; they don't want to be outdone by their peers.

Also, people often believe that others have more information about a situation than they do. So, if an investor knows that another investor is interested in your deal, they might believe that investor knows something they don't and look more favorably at the deal.

6. Use Software to Get to Know Investors

The more you know about the investors you are reaching out to, the more you can customize your communication. Investors expect you to do your research. Luckily, there are a lot of great online tools to help you learn more about your targets:

- Crystal tells you how individuals like to be emailed. Do they like short and to-the-point emails? Do they prefer friendly emails?

- Rapportive is a great Google Mail plug-in to help you see a snapshot of your investor's social profile before you hit send.

- ZoomInfo, Pipl, Klout, Data.com, and Boardex will do a biographical analysis of individuals, telling you about commonalities you can use in future outreaches.

- LinkedIn can be a powerful tool for telling you how you are connected to investors.

7. Use Social Media to Turn Cold Outreaches into Warm Leads

We've talked about how engaging with investors over social media can be a great way to add value while you're in a fundraising conversation. Social media is also a great way to establish an initial connection with investors you currently have no connection to. We spend more hours on social media than we do on email.

Finding where your target investors live online, and engaging with them on those channels, will turn cold leads into warm connections that you can reach out to directly over email.

 Hacks for Non-Valley Founders

Our final three hacks are for funders located outside Silicon Valley and other major funding hubs, like New York or Tel Aviv.

8. Make Local Investors Think You Have Valley Interest

Many entrepreneurs based outside the Valley like the idea of raising money locally, in part due to regional pride, and in part to keep their companies and their investors local for as long as possible.

But even if your goal is to raise money locally, I wouldn't recommend you start with local investors. Non-Valley investors wish they were Valley investors. Try flying to the Valley multiple times, and dropping hints locally that you are taking multiple meetings with Valley investors. Give the impression of paying little attention to local investors. Local investors will get anxious, wondering what they are missing out on. We all want what we can't have.

9. Say When You'll Be in Town, Even if You Don't Know Yet

Sometimes it can be hard to get an investor to nail down a date to meet, especially when there is no urgency. You can create urgency by stating that you are only going to be in town on a certain number of days, even if you don't have a trip booked. It will likely force an investor to act and pick a time, more so than if you said, "Let me know what works for you." It also changes the power dynamic, shifting some of the power in the conversation back to you. Once the investor confirms, book your travel.

10. Act Like You're Based in the Valley—At Least Part-Time

Silicon Valley is one of the easiest places in the world to give locals the impression that you live there. Everyone in the Valley travels a lot and is from somewhere else. Show up at all the right industry events, and be in the Valley every six weeks or so, and you'll quickly find that many people simply assume you live there.

Once people think you're local, they're much more likely to invite you to events and make introductions. While you don't want to lie about where you're based or trick investors into thinking you're based locally, the illusion of being local will help you grow a network of supporters from which to kickstart your fundraise.

Conclusion

As we bring the book to a close, I want to cover some of the key lessons I hope you'll take away with you.

Venture financing was built for high-growth businesses. Not every business will be fundable. Even for those that are fundable, venture financing is just one of a number of ways to finance a growing business. Venture capital is not right for every business and will have many lasting effects on you and your company. Be sure you know what you are getting yourself into before you accept the first check.

Fundraising is like any other sales process. You'll need great collateral and a strong sales pipeline. Running a strong sales process will not just increase your chances of success, but will also prove to investors that you are professional, organized, and knowledgeable about what it takes to close a deal.

Treat every round as if it is your last, and be mindful when spending the money you raise. The number one rule of success in startups is not to die. Fundraising is hard, and it is often harder to raise your second round than it is to raise your first round. Today, seed financing is occurring at unprecedented rates, and we're entering what has been referred to as the "Series A crunch." There is not enough Series A financing to support all of the seed-stage companies looking for their next round. Yes, great companies can always find money, but for those companies on the edge—the ones that haven't yet hit it out of the park—being self-sufficient is more important than ever.

Be sure to take advantage of all of the resources available for you at *TheEntrepreneursGuide.com*. Use the framework you've created through our templates, the exercises you've completed, and the checklists throughout the book to stay on track. Never stop learning. Use the additional resources listed on our website and available across the Web to continue honing your fundraising skills.

The real work will begin after you close your round, when you start building your business. So prepare well, hustle, get the deal done, and get back to business.

Good luck, and I look forward to seeing you over at *TheEntrepreneurs-Guide.com.*

Index

About the Author

Katherine Hague is a serial entrepreneur, an angel investor, and the founder of Female Funders (*https://www.femalefunders.com*), an online destination dedicated to inspiring and educating the next generation of female entrepreneurs and investors.

Prior to leading Female Funders, Katherine founded ShopLocket, the first preorder solution for entrepreneurs. ShopLocket was acquired in 2014 by PCH—the company behind some of your favorite tech brands and accessories.

Katherine has been named one of *FLARE* magazine's Sixty Under Thirty, one of Five Women to Watch in Wearable Tech, and one of Canada's Top 100 Most Powerful Women. She has been quoted in the *New York Times* on fashion tech and was recently interviewed for the Oprah Winfrey Network.

Find Katherine online at @KatherineHague or at *katherinehague.com*.

Get even more for your money.

Join the O'Reilly Community, and register the O'Reilly books you own. It's free, and you'll get:

- $4.99 ebook upgrade offer
- 40% upgrade offer on O'Reilly print books
- Membership discounts on books and events
- Free lifetime updates to ebooks and videos
- Multiple ebook formats, DRM FREE
- Participation in the O'Reilly community
- Newsletters
- Account management
- 100% Satisfaction Guarantee

Signing up is easy:

1. Go to: oreilly.com/go/register
2. Create an O'Reilly login.
3. Provide your address.
4. Register your books.

Note: English-language books only

To order books online:
oreilly.com/store

For questions about products or an order:
orders@oreilly.com

To sign up to get topic-specific email announcements and/or news about upcoming books, conferences, special offers, and new technologies:
elists@oreilly.com

For technical questions about book content:
booktech@oreilly.com

To submit new book proposals to our editors:
proposals@oreilly.com

O'Reilly books are available in multiple DRM-free ebook formats. For more information:
oreilly.com/ebooks

O'REILLY®